Psychology

Abnormal Psychology

BROWN
BEAR
BOOKS

Published by Brown Bear Books Limited

4877 N. Circulo Bujia
Tucson
AZ 85718
USA

First Floor
9-17 St. Albans Place
London N1 ONX

www.brownreference.com

© 2010 The Brown Reference Group Ltd

ISBN: 978-1-936333-20-2

Editorial Director: Lindsey Lowe
Managing Editor: Tim Cooke
Project Director: Laura Durman
Editor: Helen Dwyer
Designer: Barry Dwyer
Picture Researcher: Helen Dwyer

Library of Congress Cataloging-in-Publication Data available upon request

Contents

Introduction

Psychology **forms part of the Curriculum Connections series. Each of the six volumes of the set covers a particular aspect of psychology: History of Psychology; The Brain; Cognitive Development; Intellectual Development; The Individual and Society; and Abnormal Psychology.**

About this set

Each volume in *Psychology* features illustrated chapters, providing in-depth information about each subject. The chapters are all listed in the contents pages of each book. Each volume can be studied to provide a comprehensive understanding of the different aspects of psychology. However, each chapter may also be studied independently.

Within each chapter there are two key aids to learning that are to be found in color sidebars located in the margins of each page:

Curriculum Context sidebars indicate to the reader that a subject has a particular relevance to certain key state and national psychology guidelines and curricula. They highlight essential information or suggest useful ways for students to consider a subject or to include it in their studies.

Glossary sidebars define key words within the text.

At the end of the book, a summary **Glossary** lists the key terms defined in the volume. There is also a list of further print and Web-based resources and a full volume index.

Fully captioned illustrations play an important role throughout the set, including photographs and explanatory diagrams.

About this book

Abnormal Psychology examines the scientific study of psychological disorders, or "psychopathology," and asks "What is abnormality?"

People have always been affected by mental disorders that have caused distress, fear, and sometimes physical pain in sufferers or those around them. This volume shows how the number and types of abnormalities recognized as mental disorders have changed over time. It also analyzes childhood development disorders and considers how growing up with psychological difficulties affects a child's learning and socialization experiences.

As well as detailing mental disorders, *Abnormal Psychology* examines the treatments that have been administered through the centuries. These treatments have taken many forms—sometimes unusual, sometimes humane. Modern research and guidelines enable psychologists and others to diagnose and treat people suffering from mental disorders.

However, the treatments administered today still vary. Sigmund Freud pioneered the field of psychotherapy— the "talking cure"—with his theory of psychoanalysis. But many people diagnosed with mental disorders find it difficult to get counseling or psychotherapy unless they have good access to private practitioners. The majority receive medication or a form of physical therapy (a way of treating the body to relieve the symptoms of a mental disorder).

The final chapter, Mental Disorders and Society, looks at social attitudes toward psychological conditions and how they have varied throughout the 20th century. The field of psychology has made tremendous progress in developing an understanding of this complex area.

What Is Abnormality?

The scientific study of psychological disorders, or "psychopathology," is sometimes referred to as the field of abnormal psychology. The answers to major questions such as "What is abnormal?" and "What is a mental disorder?" are constantly evolving.

Terms like "abnormal" and "mental disorder" are in part defined by social and cultural beliefs, which differ from culture to culture and change over time. This is not to say that some mental disorders might not have physical causes. Many are firmly based in biology, but it is often not possible to diagnose or identify mental disorders with simple medical procedures. In many cases there may be no biological cause to detect.

Why define abnormality?

Defining psychological abnormality has many practical implications:

- It helps establish the subject matter covered by the field of abnormal psychology and so determines the patterns of human behavior that should become the subject of scientific study.
- It affects the way society thinks about and acts toward people whose behavior seems different or socially unacceptable. We usually hold people responsible for behavior that is within their control and don't hold them responsible for behavior beyond their control.
- It affects our criminal justice system: We might hold people less responsible for their crimes if we think that they have a mental disorder.
- It affects public policy: If we think people have mental disorders, we might view them as having disabilities that qualify them to receive special treatment. Defining mental abnormality also helps the government and private

organizations decide which problems are eligible for research funds.

- It affects the delivery of mental health services: Insurance companies and government health services are more likely to pay for the cost of treating emotional and behavioral problems if the problems are officially classified as psychological disorders.

Deviating from the norm

Deciding what is abnormal involves first deciding what is normal or average and then determining how far from that someone deviates. The tremendous variety of people and behaviors makes determining what is normal very difficult. Even if we could determine what is normal by developing a test of some kind, we would still have to decide how far from the average people's thoughts, feelings, and behaviors must be for them to be abnormal.

Another problem with defining psychological abnormality as deviating from the norm is that someone can greatly differ from the average in a way that is useful instead of harmful or desirable instead of undesirable. For example, people whose intelligence is much higher than average have advantages over those whose intelligence is much lower than average.

Curriculum Context

Students may find it useful to consider at what point normal behavior becomes abnormal in a variety of situations.

How Common Are Psychological Disorders?

How many people are abnormal? How many suffer from psychological or mental disorders? One of the most famous studies of mental disorders in the United States was the Epidemiologic Catchment Area Study (ECA). It was conducted over more than 10 years and involved more than 19,000 participants; the results were published in 1991. The researchers used the 1980 edition of the *Diagnostic and Statistical Manual* to determine whether a person had a disorder. They found that 32 percent of adults had met the criteria for at least one mental disorder at some point in their lives. They also found that 20 percent could be diagnosed with a disorder at the time of the study.

Abnormal as maladaptive

Since defining abnormal behavior in terms of deviance from norms can be problematic, many psychologists look at how a person's behavior affects their own well-being and that of the social group. Behavior is considered maladaptive if it has a negative effect on society or on a person's ability to function in society. For example, a seriously underweight woman suffering from an eating disorder is behaving maladaptively since her behavior affects her health. A paranoid man who plots to kill random people is behaving maladaptively in a way that harms others, not himself.

If your behavior helps you cope with stress, deal with challenge, or accomplish your goals, then your behavior is termed adaptive. Behaving adaptively includes the ability to know when your behavior is not working well and to come up with a new way of trying to solve a problem. For example, if you fail an exam, you might decide that you need to study differently, find a tutor, or talk to a counselor. These are examples of adaptive responses. Doing nothing, blaming the teacher, and simply "hoping for the best" are examples of maladaptive responses. Becoming so distressed that you cannot think clearly about what to do is also an example of a maladaptive response. In general, behaving adaptively means learning from experience and being flexible in how you deal with life's challenges.

Maladaptive
Not adjusting appropriately to a situation.

Adaptiveness depends on the standards set by a culture. Since the late 20th century the ideal of female beauty in Western societies has been represented by ultraslim models. Women who adopt a strict diet to maintain slim figures might be considered adaptive in such cultures but maladaptive in others. Maladaptiveness is also a matter of degree, however. So, if a woman diets to the extent that she damages her health, then her behavior is maladaptive.

Cultural demands

Whether or not your behavior is adaptive depends on what goals you are trying to accomplish and whether or not your culture approves of those goals. For example, a person who fasts for religious reasons is not displaying maladaptive behavior according to most cultures. On the other hand, a person who is already thin but refuses to eat because they believe that they are overweight is displaying maladaptive behavior.

Fast

To abstain from food or drink, especially as a religious observance.

Degree of maladaptiveness

Most people behave maladaptively sometimes, but it is the extent to which that behavior is damaging to the person's or the society's well-being that matters. Each culture's judgments about which behaviors are adaptive or maladaptive always involve the culture's values, its deeply held beliefs about what is right or wrong, what it means to be a good person or a good citizen, and what it means to lead a good life.

Curriculum Context

Students might like to gather examples of behavior that is considered abnormal in cultures different from their own.

Abnormal as distressed

One of the factors that psychologists consider when assessing people for abnormality is the degree of distress they experience. Distress can take many forms, including sadness, anxiety, anger, loss of appetite, and irritability. It is important to consider distress as a factor in defining abnormality, because feeling depressed or anxious can be a painful or unpleasant experience. Distress is also important because it can interfere with our ability to function effectively in daily life: It can be maladaptive. In many situations, however, distress is normal.

A problem with using distress as a sign of abnormality is that we are still left with two difficult questions: How much distress in a given situation should we consider to be too much? How long need someone's distress continue before it is termed maladaptive?

Another problem with the distress definition is that not all examples of abnormal behavior or mental disorders are accompanied by distress. People with antisocial personality disorder do not feel remorse or distress for the many times that they lie, cheat, steal, and otherwise use people for their own personal pleasure or profit.

Social acceptability

Many behaviors are considered normal because they conform to social standards of acceptable or good behavior. Similarly, behaviors that deviate from socially acceptable actions might be considered abnormal. Some behaviors are considered normal and adaptive because they help people get along better and make everyday life more orderly and predictable.

Conformity

Compliance with laws, rules, or standards.

While conformity is useful, too much conformity or conformity to the wrong beliefs and practices can be maladaptive, not only for the individual but also for society. A person who is constantly worried about whether or not what they do or how they appear is approved of by others is not a psychologically healthy person. A little nonconformity can be healthy for us. It can also be healthy for society.

Curriculum Context

Students should be able to provide historical examples of behavior that was considered abnormal at the time but which today seems normal.

Sometimes people violate social norms because of deeply held beliefs that such norms are wrong. For this reason, some violations of social beliefs and practices can be viewed as acts of courage. When Rosa Parks refused in 1955 to give up her bus seat to a white passenger in Alabama, she helped begin the Civil Rights movement in the United States. Without such violators of contemporary social norms, a society and its culture would remain static and possibly steeped in injustice. Science and art are also advanced by daring people who defy the status quo. For example, Galileo defied the Catholic Church by insisting that the Sun, not Earth, was the center of our solar system.

Abnormal as disordered

Do the people we consider psychologically abnormal have some kind of disorder that makes them abnormal? The answer to this question depends on how we define disorder. We can use the term "disorder" simply to refer to a pattern of thinking, feeling, and behaving that is generally maladaptive. In other words, it is disordered because it disrupts the order in the lives of the person and other people.

The DSM

The *Diagnostic and Statistical Manual* (DSM) is accepted by most mental health professionals as the standard and official classification of mental disorders, especially in the United States and the United Kingdom. First published by the American Psychiatric Association in 1952 and on its fourth revised edition by the year 2000, the DSM provides the organizational structure for almost every textbook and course on the study of abnormal psychology for undergraduate and graduate students. It also provides the basis for almost every professional book on the assessment and treatment of psychological problems.

The DSM basically groups psychological disorders into categories. Mental health professionals use the categories to agree on a common diagnosis, while researchers use them to guide them in their studies and insurance companies use them to determine how to reimburse patients and providers for mental health services, such as psychotherapy and medication.

The DSM definition

The American Psychiatric Association (APA) provides an official definition of "mental disorder" in the DSM as:

"A clinically significant behavioral or psychological syndrome or pattern that occurs in an individual and that is associated with present distress, for example, a painful symptom, or disability, that is, impairment in one or more important areas of functioning, or with a significantly increased risk of suffering, death, pain, disability, or an important loss of freedom. In addition, this syndrome or pattern must not be merely an expectable and culturally sanctioned response to a particular event

Syndrome
A condition characterized by a set of associated symptoms.

Sanctioned
Given official permission or approval.

[and] must currently be considered a manifestation of a behavioral, psychological, or biological dysfunction in the individual."

This definition indicates that we need to consider a person's culture when determining whether or not that person's behavior is abnormal. The DSM also avoids the use of the terms "illness" or "disease." Instead, it talks of "mental disorders," which are those psychological conditions that make people distressed, disabled, and at increased risk of harm, regardless of whether the cause is clearly a biological disease or not.

Scientific or social?

The number of pages in the DSM has increased from 86 in 1952 to over 900 in 2000, and the number of mental disorders increased from 106 to 297. As the boundaries of mental disorder have expanded with each DSM revision, many everyday life problems have been pathologized, or turned into disorders, and the sheer number of people with diagnosable mental disorders has continued to grow. For example, many common difficulties are now considered abnormal, such as children's

A firefighter in action. Some people in occupations involving life-threatening circumstances might be diagnosed with post–traumatic stress disorder. PTSD has only been recognized in the DSM as a mental disorder since 1980.

temper tantrums, being drunk, not desiring or enjoying sex, and learning difficulties.

Models of abnormality

Abnormal psychologists recognize various models of mental disorder that describe the underlying causes of abnormalities or recommend how to treat them. Different psychologists might routinely apply certain models, while others view more than one model as valid. Some psychologists have developed models that integrate all possible causes of mental disorders.

Medical model

The medical model views psychological abnormality as similar to a disease: something inside a person that causes them problems and distress. This model assumes that people with psychological problems have illnesses with specific symptoms, causes, and cures. The model works well for mental disorders that have a known and testable cause, such as many dementias, for example. These disorders involve deterioration of mental abilities, which can sometimes be measured in the shrinking of brain disease and the loss of brain cells. Alzheimer's disease involves characteristic plaques and nerve tangles in the brain, but it is not known whether they are a cause or consequence of the disease. Researchers working within the medical model have located specific genes that may be responsible for the disease. However, researchers often spend a great deal of time looking for such causes. Not only do they study genetics, but they also consider how the brain works and the role of brain chemicals.

Psychological models of abnormality

Many psychological problems are difficult to diagnose and treat if a simple medical model is followed, though. Take anxiety, for example. Each of us feels different amounts of anxiety at different times depending on the situation.

Curriculum Context

Students should be aware of how the major mental disorders are defined in the *Diagnostic and Statistical Manual*.

Gene

A unit of heredity that determines some specific characteristic and that is passed from parent to offspring.

Psychodynamic models of disorder attempt to redress this problem by considering the mental, rather than the physical, origins of problems. The pioneer of psychoanalysis, Sigmund Freud, believed that mental disorders were largely due to conflicts between different aspects of the personality: the id, ego, and superego. Some of these conflicts, he suggested, might have remained unresolved since childhood. Freud developed psychoanalysis to treat mental disorders. This psychoanalytical model of mental disorder is one type of psychodynamic model. The psychoanalytical model has been criticized for the lack of experimental support and scientific rigor and for its simplistic view of life.

Other psychological theories of mental disorder include the behaviorial, or learning, model. This model focuses on fixing the behavioral problem itself rather than on its possible causes, which are the focus of psychodynamic models. Cognitive models of mental disorder focus on the thoughts, processes, and feelings that accompany mental disorders.

Religion versus Science

Throughout history, people have explained psychological abnormality mainly in terms of magic, religion, or—most recently—science. Documents show that the ancient Egyptians, Chinese, Hebrews, and Greeks believed that abnormal behavior was caused by demons, spirits, or gods, depending on the religious beliefs of the people. For example, God might punish people for sinful acts by taking away their ability to think rationally and by making them behave in bizarre ways. Those who believed that abnormality was caused by an evil spirit that possessed a person's body might summon a priest to exorcise the spirit.

Exorcisms could involve reciting chants, prayers, and performing rituals, such as whipping the evil spirit out of the person's body or making the person drink potions.

During the 18th and 19th centuries in Europe, huge advances were made in science and the scientific method. Scientists emphasized rational thought and scientific discovery through careful observation and experimentation. Early psychologists adopted scientific methodology and began the process of turning psychology into a science, which included diagnosing, classifying, and treating mental disorders.

Social construction "model"

A particularly challenging model of mental disorder is that proposed by social constructionists. Social constructions are ideas that societies build over time. Social constructionists say that we create our reality through our attitudes, beliefs, and feelings, which are always changing.

Members of a culture define what is normal and abnormal by sharing ideas and engaging in formal and informal debates. All of us take part in this discourse, and so we all influence the definitions of such terms as "beauty," "justice," and "abnormality." In addition, we are all influenced by these definitions, because how our culture defines these terms influences how people in our culture think about each other and behave toward each other.

Cultural considerations

The mental disorders in the DSM are defined by North American psychiatrists following Western concepts of disorder, normality, and abnormality. The definitions do not always work in other cultures. Certain disorders are unique to particular cultures. They are called culture-bound disorders. The existence of culture-bound disorders suggests that psychological, social, and other nonphysical factors are very important in the onset and origin of mental disorders.

This young woman proudly sports tattoos and piercings, which might in the past have been seen as a sign of mental disorder. Today, however, the practice is increasingly common and is not considered abnormal.

Mental Disorders

People have always been affected by mental disorders. Throughout history the treatment of disorders has taken many forms. With the growth of modern research, clinicians diagnose more mental disorders than ever before.

Ancient Greek and Roman philosophers and physicians described a number of such disorders. They principally were: melancholia (sadness); mania (frenzied activity); delusions (blatantly false beliefs); hysteria; and hallucinations (imagined sights and sounds). Before the fifth century B.C., Greeks generally believed that diseases and mental disorders were caused by gods, spirits, or demons. But then the physician Hippocrates proposed that diseases, including mental disorders, are rooted in physical, or natural, causes.

Medieval madness

During the medieval period in Europe, the idea that the world was a battleground between God and the devil led to beliefs that people showing unusual behaviors were possessed by devils or evil spirits. The cure for mania, for example, would be to expel the demons that possessed the sufferer. Clergymen administering such treatment would chant and pray to exorcise the evil spirits. They might even order the destruction of the body in order to save the soul.

From the 15th to the 17th centuries, mental disorders became equated with physical ailments. However, treatment was still primitive and barbaric. The asylums that were built were often vast institutions that grew increasingly crowded. Standards of hygiene were low, and care and conditions were inhumane.

Moral treatment

During the 18th century there was, in some countries, a marked improvement in the treatment of the

Hysteria

Physical ailments with no apparent cause, but thought to be related to the possession of a uterus and, therefore, exclusive to women.

Exorcise

To attempt to drive out an evil spirit.

mentally ill. In the United States, Benjamin Rush (1745–1813) encouraged hospitals to employ only caring, intelligent, and considerate staff to work with patients. Carers would be encouraged to read to patients, talk with them, and take them on walks.

Bedlam

The Hospital of St. Mary of Bethlehem—possibly the world's first asylum for the mentally disordered—was originally set up as a priory in London, England, in 1247. It became a hospital for the mentally disordered in 1402 and was given to the City of London by King Henry VIII in 1547. "Bethlehem," soon contracted to "Bethlem," became "bedlam," a generic term for all asylums and popularly used to mean chaos or uproar. The hospital became a popular tourist attraction, and people from all over Europe would come to stare at the inmates. Today the Bethlehem Royal Hospital still functions as a psychiatric hospital, now relocated in southern England.

Somatogenic or psychogenic?

From the late 19th to the early 20th centuries, two other views of mental disorders emerged. Emil Kraepelin (1856–1926) revived the idea that psychological abnormality has physical causes, a view known as the somatogenic perspective or the medical model. The other view is called the psychogenic model or psychogenic perspective. According to this model, psychological problems can cause physical ailments.

The medical model

Mental symptoms, or abnormal behaviors, are identified, grouped together, classified, and investigated to find effective treatments for them. The first detailed attempt to classify abnormal behavior was undertaken in 1913 by Emil Kraepelin. After observing hospital patients, he suggested that there were 18 types of mental disorder, each with a characteristic pattern of symptoms (a syndrome). Each syndrome took a particular course, had particular causes, and had a characteristic outcome. Kraepelin's work led to the development of two further classification systems. These systems are still in wide use today and are known as the *International Standard Classification of Diseases, Injuries, and Causes of Death* (ICD)' and the *Diagnostic and Statistical Manual* (DSM). The following sections discuss some of the most common and familiar mental disorders classified in the DSM.

Anxiety disorders

Anxiety is a common emotion that involves a general feeling of worry or fear and affects our physical well-being, behavior, and thoughts. It is often a normal response to challenging situations and can act as a motivator or protective mechanism.

Curriculum Context

Students should be able to distinguish between state and trait anxiety.

Psychologists often make a distinction between two types of anxiety: state and trait. State anxiety varies according to the situation with which the person is faced. Trait anxiety is relatively constant over time and refers to a person's general predisposition, or vulnerability, to anxiety. Anxiety disorders are mainly treated by behavior and cognitive therapies, as well as psychoanalytic psychotherapy. Medication may help the person cope with the anxiety, but it will not cure it.

Panic disorder

Panic disorder is when someone experiences sudden and repeated physical discomfort caused by fear. The symptoms include shortness of breath, dizziness, nausea, and anxiety about losing control or going crazy. The person experiences these intense symptoms in short bouts. These attacks often lead to the development of anticipatory anxiety, that is, a fear that further attacks will occur. Panic disorder can be accompanied by agoraphobia.

Agoraphobia

The extreme or irrational fear of being alone and helpless in an inescapable situation; it is especially characterized by fear of open or public places.

Phobia

An extreme or irrational fear of something.

Specific phobias

A fear develops into a specific phobia when the amount of danger attached to a particular object and the harm

In the traditional nursery rhyme "Little Miss Muffet" a spider "frightened Miss Muffet away." Fear of spiders, or arachnophobia, is a common specific phobia. Cognitive behavioral therapy might have helped Miss Muffet.

it can cause are magnified. When encountering the feared object or situation, the individual experiences an increase in physical anxiety reactions and tries to escape.

Social phobias

People often experience a certain level of anxiety in social settings, but sometimes this fear becomes so great that a social phobia develops. It involves a dread of public rejection or embarrassment. People with such phobias often avoid situations in which they might be the center of attention. They might fear blushing in front of others, being watched, or choking on food when eating in public places.

Generalized anxiety disorder

Generalized anxiety disorder (GAD) is excessive, long-term worry. It is caused by fears of not being able to cope, failure, rejection, or death. The person also experiences physical symptoms, including increased muscle tension, sensitivity, a high breathing rate, and increased arousal levels, such as a racing heartbeat.

Post–traumatic stress disorder

Post–traumatic stress disorder (PTSD) refers to a range of symptoms that people might experience after they have been involved in violent or catastrophic events that have stressed and frightened them. Symptoms of the condition include repetitive and distressing thoughts about the incident and flashbacks, sleep disturbance, irritability, and a sense of isolation. PTSD can occur at any time between one week and 30 years after the traumatic event. It is most likely to occur in individuals who are single, divorced, or widowed, or in people who are socially withdrawn.

Obsessive–compulsive disorder

Obsessive–compulsive disorder (OCD) is a long-term and disabling condition characterized by the experience of persistent thoughts (obsessions) that result in anxiety and repetitive actions. The person feels compelled to perform the actions (compulsions) over and over to avoid anxiety. Common compulsions include hand washing, persistent cleaning, and checking behaviors.

Biological theories

Biological theories of anxiety disorders focus on the effects of chemical and physical changes within the brain. When neurotransmitters are released in the brain, they stimulate the autonomic nervous system, causing changes in heart rate, breathing, and muscle tension. People with anxiety disorders might have excessive responses to stimulation of the autonomic nervous system. For example, some people with PTSD have higher levels of the neurotransmitter norepinephrine than the rest of the population, making them more aroused and alert to danger.

Genetic theories

Many studies of families and twins have shown a tendency for the disorders to be inherited. Studies of twins estimate that between 30 and 90 percent of identical twins will develop an anxiety disorder if their twin is similarly affected. Research suggests that certain environmental conditions must also be present for a disorder to develop.

Behavioral theories

Behaviorists take the view that some people can acquire anxiety disorders because they associate fear

Neurotransmitters
The chemicals that transfer impulses from one nerve fiber to another.

Autonomic nervous system
The communication network by which the brain controls all parts of the body except for contraction of skeletal muscles.

with something that in itself would not provoke anxiety. They then reinforce the fear by associating it with other situations or objects and by making a habit of avoiding the feared object.

Behavioral theorists propose that anxiety is maintained by operant conditioning. For example, when a person who suffers from obsessive-compulsive disorder keeps repeating certain behaviors, the repetition reduces the original fear because the expected consequences of not performing the actions do not take place. Anxiety levels that rise when the obsessional thoughts or images occur might be reduced if the person carries out a certain action or thinks a particular thought.

Curriculum Context

Many curricula ask students to design procedures to produce operant responses.

Cognitive theories

Cognitive theories explain anxiety disorders in terms of the connection between emotional responses and thought processes. Incorrect interpretations of a situation are the main factors considered in cognitive theories of anxiety. Aaron Beck noted that socially anxious people are more aware of how they appear to others and are highly sensitive to feedback or criticism. Beck also noted that people who experience panic attacks consistently overestimate the significance of the physical sensations they experience. As the symptoms of anxiety occur, they make a series of misinterpretations and overestimate the threat. This

In a study of phobias, people were shown a series of images of either snakes or flowers. Following each image, they either felt an electric shock, or heard a tone, or nothing happened to them. At the end of the experiment, those who were frightened of snakes thought that most of the electric shocks had been administered when snakes were shown, even though the three stimuli occurred with equal regularity across all the images. The subjects overemphasized the connection between the image of the snake and the electric shock.

leads to an increase in the physical symptoms being experienced and the likelihood of a panic attack.

Schizophrenia

Schizophrenia has been recognized only for the last 100 years or so. Emil Kraepelin observed the behavior of many of his mentally ill patients over long periods and put forward the first of his findings in 1898. The main characteristics of the disorder were delusions, hallucinations, negativism, attentional difficulties, stereotyped behaviors, and emotional dysfunction.

Symptoms

Clinicians have attempted to group the symptoms of schizophrenia into three broad categories: positive symptoms, negative symptoms, and psychomotor (movement) symptoms. Among the positive symptoms are delusions, disorganized thinking and speech, and hallucinations.

Delusions are ideas that people strongly believe in but that have no obvious basis in fact. Some people diagnosed with schizophrenia have a single delusion that dominates their lives; others have a range of different delusions. Delusions of persecution occur when people feel that the whole world is out to get them. Delusions of reference attach a particular meaning to the behaviors of others. Delusions of grandeur occur, for example, when people believe themselves to be a famous person when they obviously are not or that they can do impossible things. Delusions of

Hallucinations

Perceptions of objects, people, or events that have no basis in reality.

In 1911 Eugene Bleuler explained that he had named the disorder schizophrenia: *"because . . . the 'splitting' of the different psychic functions is one of its most important characteristics."*

control occur when people believe that all their actions are governed by external forces, such as radio signals or aliens from outer space.

Disorganized thinking and speech occur when a person switches illogically from one topic to another. The person might make incoherent links and suffer great confusion. Some people diagnosed with schizophrenia use neologisms, or they use words in ways that make no sense. They might also perseverate.

Neologisms
Made-up, private words that others cannot understand without explanation.

Perseverate
To repeat words or phrases again and again.

People diagnosed with schizophrenia often report heightened perception. Some are overcome by the sights and sounds around them, so it is impossible for them to organize them in their mind and to focus on any specific event or thought. All five senses can be involved in hallucinations.

Negative symptoms of schizophrenia are those that show an absence of adequate behaviors. One of the main examples is poor speech. Psychomotor symptoms include a lack of control over movement and the development of odd grimaces and mannerisms that are often repetitive and might seem purposeful.

Types of schizophrenia

Psychiatrists have tried to classify the disorder by separating it into different types. Hebephrenic schizophrenia is the most severe form of the disorder. It is usually diagnosed in childhood or early adolescence. It is thought to last a lifetime, and the symptoms tend to get worse over time. The main characteristics are incoherent language, vivid hallucinations that are often sexual or religious in their content, disorganized delusions, and extreme social withdrawal.

Catatonic
Immobile or unresponsive.

People who have catatonic schizophrenia can hold set positions for long periods without moving. Their limbs grow stiff and might become swollen from lack of

Somatoform Disorders

Somatoform disorders are characterized by physical symptoms that suggest a medical cause but are not fully explained by any medical condition. Often, investigation reveals that the causes are psychological, not physical. However, this does not mean that the symptoms are under the person's control, in contrast to factitious disorders. The two best-known types of somatoform disorders are sometimes called hysteria and hypochondria.

Hypochondria (or Briquet's syndrome) is now more likely to be called somatization disorder. Sufferers report feeling pain in many different parts of their body. The condition is relatively common and occurs in about 1 percent of adult women. It is very unusual for men to have this disorder. The onset of this disorder is generally before the age of 30.

Hysteria, or conversion disorder, involves unexplained physical symptoms that affect voluntary motor functions (control of bodily movements) in a way that suggests the functioning of the nervous system has been affected, though evidence of any damage cannot be found and is probably not present. Symptoms include tics, tremors, "pins and needles," blindness, deafness, and loss of sensation in or paralysis of arms or legs.

movement. Some victims become mute. Although they might be aware of what is being said around them, they are unable to respond. Other sufferers are agitated and move in wild, uncontrollable, excited ways.

Paranoid
Unreasonably or obsessively anxious, suspicious, or mistrustful.

The strongest characteristic of paranoid schizophrenia is the presence of a highly organized and thought-out delusional belief system. People diagnosed with paranoid schizophrenia often appear to be fully functioning, but they might be either contemptuous of or angered by those who do not share their delusions.

It is impossible to look at schizophrenia without considering the biological, psychological, and social factors that contribute to its development.

Medical models
If you have one parent diagnosed with schizophrenia, though, your chance of being diagnosed with it increases to one in five. If both your parents are

diagnosed with schizophrenia, your chance of being diagnosed increases to one in two or three. Many studies have been carried out on pairs of twins. They have found a higher incidence of schizophrenia in identical twins than in fraternal twins. Other studies have found a higher incidence in adopted children who are placed with parents with schizophrenia. So although genetic factors do play an important role, there must still be some environmental factors at work.

Scientists have closely studied biochemical influences in schizophrenia. According to one theory, some people inherit metabolic problems. Because of these errors in functioning, their bodies break down naturally occurring chemicals into toxic ones that produce schizophrenic symptoms.

The dopamine hypothesis proposes that schizophrenia is caused by overactive synapses. People diagnosed with schizophrenia are thought to have numerous or densely packed receptor sites for the neurotransmitter dopamine. In experiments in which people not diagnosed with schizophrenia were given certain drugs which increase dopamine levels, they showed symptoms identical to those of schizophrenia. Similarly, drugs that block the dopamine receptors tend to reduce schizophrenic symptoms. Other studies have suggested that the positive symptoms of schizophrenia might have a single cause that is related to dopamine, while negative symptoms might have some other cause related to brain damage.

The psychoanalytic view

The psychoanalytic view suggests that schizophrenia develops when the ego has problems in distinguishing between the self and the real world. Sigmund Freud (1856–1939) proposed that the two key processes involved in schizophrenia were regression to a pre-ego state, followed by attempts to reestablish ego control.

Biochemical
Concerned with the chemical processes that occur within living organisms.

Metabolic
Concerning the chemical processes within an organism that maintain life.

Synapses
The junctions between nerve cells in the brain.

Ego
The part of the psyche that distinguishes between the self and the real world.

He believed that schizophrenia resulted from conflict between a person's self-gratifying impulses and the demands of the real world. When the external world seems harsh or hostile, people regress to an earlier period in their functioning. Regression takes them to a place of primary narcissism, similar to that of infants who feel only their own needs.

The behaviorist view
Behaviorists generally propose that people are taught to behave in certain ways by their families, friends, and environmental contacts. Most people are able to attend to social cues, such as smiling and body language. Behaviorists suggest that people diagnosed with schizophrenia have not had the opportunity to learn these social norms.

Instead of focusing on social cues, some people are thought to pay too much attention to extraneous inputs, such as the noise level in a room. Attention to these other cues might be reinforced, and so this behavior is likely to recur. Experiments in which people diagnosed with schizophrenia are offered rewards or reinforcement for socially acceptable conduct have shown that such behaviors can be taught.

The family view
The double-bind hypothesis was put forward by Gregory Bateson (1904–1980). According to the theory, parents repeatedly send contradictory messages that put their children in a double bind. For example, the primary communication in words might be the opposite of the metacommunication (the tone, gestures, and context) of the message. Because of the contradiction, the children cannot be sure what their parents are really telling them. The views and behaviors that such children might adopt to cope with their environment might well be seen as schizophrenic symptoms.

Narcissism
Extreme selfishness, with a grandiose view of one's own talents and a craving for admiration.

Hypothesis
A proposed explanation based on limited evidence and used as the starting point for further investigation.

Most people suffering from depression find it difficult to get a good night's sleep. They might find it difficult to get to sleep or to sleep all through the night.

Mood disorders

Mood disorders are a group of conditions in which the person experiences significant emotional disturbance. They affect how people think about themselves, interact with others, work, and plan their lives.

Depression

Depression is a term used to describe a mood state in which the main features include prolonged feelings of sadness or emptiness and lack of interest in previously enjoyed activities. Depressed people often have difficulty spending time with other people and might lose contact with friends and family. They might even lose their job because of poor work performance.

Depression can also result from medical conditions or other psychological disorders. For example, people suffering from adrenal and thyroid dysfunction often display depressive symptoms due to their being either very over- or underweight. Similarly, agoraphobics might become depressed because their fear of being vulnerable in public places makes it difficult for them to experience taking part in social activities.

Adrenal
Relating to a pair of ductless glands above the kidneys.

Thyroid
A large, ductless gland in the neck.

Agoraphobics
People with an extreme or irrational fear of being alone and helpless in an inescapable situation; they are often afraid of open or public places.

Typical symptoms

The typical emotions experienced during depression include sadness, guilt, and despair. It is also common for a depressed person to experience irritability, agitation, and anxiety. As the depression becomes worse, they might not bother to eat or cook for themselves, stop going to work, or taking care of their appearance. Sometimes depression makes people not want to live, and they might contemplate, attempt, or even commit suicide.

The effects of depression on a person's thinking include indecisiveness, reduced concentration, and decreased speed of thought. Sufferers often feel that others do not understand them or are punishing them, and they do not look forward to the future.

Depression can also cause changes in the sufferer's psychomotor activity (movements). The changes can range from slowed movements or lack of movement to restless activity, such as pacing up and down. Depression causes a range of changes in physiological, or body, functioning, such as reduced or increased appetite, fatigue or excessive tiredness, and loss of sex drive. Sleep disturbance has been estimated to affect more than 90 percent of depressed individuals. The average age for the development of depression is 40, but there is mounting evidence that depression is beginning to affect people at increasingly younger ages.

Biological factors

Biological factors that influence the development of depression include changes in neurotransmitter levels within the brain. Neurotransmitters carry chemical messages between neurons (nerve cells) and can influence mood and behavior. Research has generally focused on three types of neurotransmitter: serotonin, dopamine, and norepinephrine. These particular neurotransmitters assist in the regulation of emotions,

Curriculum Context

Students should be aware of the ways in which mental states can trigger biological changes.

Curriculum Context

Students should understand the extent to which body chemistry can affect how people feel, both mentally and physically.

Cognitive Errors or Biases in Depression

People with depression usually have a low opinion of themselves. Below are four examples of cognitive mistakes they frequently make.

Overgeneralization
A gross generalization based on a single event.
Situation: Being unable to answer a question asked by a teacher.
Thought: "I'm going to fail the rest of the year."

Black-and-white (all-or-nothing) thinking
Taking an extreme view of a situation.
Situation: Getting a test back and achieving 70 percent.
Thought: "If I don't get 100 percent, I'm a total failure."

Arbitrary inference
Drawing a conclusion from an event or situation when there is a lack of evidence to support this conclusion.
Situation: Waiters in a restaurant forget to take your dinner order.
Thought: "They're ignoring me; I'm obviously not worth their time."

Magnification/minimization
Exaggerating or ignoring a particular aspect of a situation.
Situation: A woman finds out she hasn't been invited to a friend's party.
Thought: "They obviously don't like me anymore. I must be a bad person."

including stress, sleep functions, and appetite. All three are often found at low levels in depressed people.

Much of the research into the changes in neurotransmitter levels in depression has focused on the action of antidepressant medications that assist in the regulation of neurotransmitters in the brain. For example, the medication fluoxetine (trade name, Prozac) alters the levels of serotonin being passed through the brain. Its use has been shown to result in a reduction of depressive symptoms.

Genetic factors
Researchers who have studied the frequency of depression among family members have estimated that people are between one and a half and three times more likely to develop depression if one of their parents or siblings has the disorder. Also, twin studies

have shown that if one identical twin develops depression, the chances of the other twin developing the disorder can be as high as 75 percent.

Psychological theories

The fact that the rate of depression in identical twins is not 100 percent indicates that other factors influence the possibility of depression developing. Psychological theories of depression consider these factors as important in the development of the disorder. They focus on sufferers' subjective experiences and how they interpret the events that occur in their lives.

Sigmund Freud suggested that depression occurs as a result of anger being turned inward, especially after the loss (real or imagined) of a valued family member or friend. Freud stated that this internally directed anger leads to self-criticism and blame, and that the aim of the treatment is to release this anger.

Psychoanalytic explanations such as Freud's have been criticized by other theorists. Depression can affect people who have not suffered the loss of a loved one. Also, according to Freud, the dreams of depressed people should have themes of anger, violence, or rage. In fact, the dreams of depressed people tend to center on failure and loss.

Some of the latest psychoanalytic theories of depression propose that it develops when people believe they have not reached their true potential. The result is a general feeling of helplessness and low self-esteem that leads to depression.

Interpersonal theories

Interpersonal theories suggest that depressed people have poorer social skills than other people. People experiencing depression have also been observed to have poor problem-solving skills and to make poor

Subjective

Influenced by personal feelings or opinions.

Curriculum Context

Many curricula expect students to contrast psychoanalytic explanations of depression with biological, social, and cognitive explanations.

day-to-day decisions. Additional research has shown that depressed people are more likely to be rejected by their friends or peers. It has been suggested that they might reject participation in enjoyable activities, talk about their negative experiences, or engage in conflict with others because they are irritable. Such reactions lead to social isolation as others begin to avoid them.

Cognitive theories

Cognitive theories suggest that depression is caused by the negative misinterpretations people make about themselves, their world, and the future. Aaron Beck observed that depressed people tend to make specific errors in their thinking and develop specific beliefs with strong negative elements based on these thought errors. Beck also suggested that information that did not fit with these beliefs was ignored or considered irrelevant. Beck concluded that people's negative beliefs are about the self, the world, and the future. He called this the cognitive triad. There has been some criticism of the theory that depressed

"Laugh and the world laughs with you." Depressed people can alienate others. Because of their depression they might prefer not to join in with social activities, and people might reject them because they feel that they cannot enjoy themselves in the company of someone who is depressed.

individuals make cognitive errors. That is because it has been shown that in some situations depressed people make more accurate interpretations of their situation than nondepressed people.

Helplessness theories

Helplessness theories of depression explore the specific thoughts of an individual when depressed. The concept of learned helplessness was demonstrated in experiments conducted by Martin Seligman, who observed that animals that received repeated electric shocks from which they could not escape became passive and eventually stopped trying to avoid the shocks. Seligman likened this to the development of depression in people. That is, sufferers believe that they have little control over their lives and become passive.

Bipolar 1 disorder

Another type of mood disorder that features depression is known as bipolar 1 disorder. It was first described as manic depression by Emil Kraepelin in 1899 because it is characterized by periods of both depression and mania (excitement). The typical emotions experienced during a manic episode include elation, euphoria, irritability, and impatience. The sufferer typically becomes very sociable. Mania often increases a person's level of motivation. Impulsive behavior is very common. The cognitive aspects of mania include racing thoughts and flights of ideas. Sufferers have difficulty keeping to one line of thought and randomly and quickly talk about a range of topics. It is often characterized by excessive levels of activity and less sleep than usual. Appetite tends to fluctuate, and sufferers may have an increased sex drive. Mania usually gives sufferers increased self-confidence or a belief that they have special talents or abilities.

Psychiatrists think that certain neurotransmitters are involved in the development of bipolar 1 disorder.

Curriculum Context

Students may be asked to explain how animal models of abnormality offer insights into human problems.

Euphoria
A state of intense excitement or happiness.

They have found norepinephrine to be low in depressed people and high in people experiencing a manic episode. Fluctuating levels of this chemical messenger might cause the cycle between depression and mania. Researchers have also found that fluctuations in serotonin alter levels of other neurotransmitters in the brain, possibly triggering the start of a manic or depressive episode.

Bipolar 1 disorder has a strong genetic basis. Research indicates that the children of sufferers are between 8 and 18 times more likely to develop the disorder. Twin studies have also shown a genetic link. Other theorists suggest that bipolar 1 disorder is a defense mechanism against stressful life events.

Eating disorders

Psychiatrists and psychologists generally tend to divide eating disorders into two broad categories: anorexia nervosa and bulimia nervosa. There is a lot of overlap in the behavioral characteristics and psychological processes of each.

Anorexia nervosa

People with anorexia nervosa do not lose their appetites but are often hungry and preoccupied with food. They want to eat but seem to be starving themselves. Anorexics might even love to cook for others, but they avoid eating any calorie-rich foods themselves. They usually have a distorted body image, thinking they are fat when they are wasting away.

During a manic episode a person with bipolar disorder might indulge in impractical impulse behavior, such as going on an unaffordable shopping spree.

People are diagnosed as anorexic if they weigh less than 85 percent of the expected weight for their age and height in normal circumstances. They might look extremely thin and feeble and they often have other health problems, including low blood pressure, constipation, dehydration, and low body temperature.

For every male sufferer there are 15 females who have the disorder. However, there is evidence that the number of men with eating disorders is rapidly increasing. Anorexia usually starts at between 14 and 16 years, although cases of anorexia in children as young as eight years old have been reported. It is estimated that between 5 and 15 percent of people with anorexia die from it or from related disorders.

Bulimia nervosa

Bulimia nervosa is characterized by sporadic episodes of compulsive binge eating. People with bulimia rapidly eat lots of carbohydrate-rich foods in a seemingly uncontrolled way. Bulimics do not stop to taste the food. The binge usually ends with stomach pains or some kind of purging—either self-induced vomiting or defecating as a result of taking laxatives. It is the severity and frequency of the binge eating in bulimia that makes it such a severe disorder. In mild cases, a person might binge two or three times a week. In more extreme cases, it might occur 30 times a week.

The process of bingeing and purging has all sorts of side effects. Bulimia sufferers often have puffy cheeks, because vomiting swells the parotid glands in the lower jaw. Tooth enamel can often decay because of the acid brought up when vomiting. Sufferers also have digestive tract problems, dehydration, anxiety, depression, and sleep disturbance.

There is no single theory that can explain why people experience anorexia and bulimia. There are many

Curriculum Context

Students may find it useful to contrast the symptoms of and mental states accompanying anorexia and bulimia.

Parotid glands

A pair of large salivary glands just in front of each ear.

People who suffer from bulimia first indulge in carbohydrate-rich foods, such as burgers, and then force themselves to throw up in order to lose the calories.

biological, psychodynamic, family, and sociocultural theories that, when combined, can provide some understanding of what is happening.

Biological theories

Some theorists have suggested that anorexia is caused by damage to various parts of the hypothalamus, the part of the brain that helps balance, monitors bodily functions, and controls the endocrine system via the pituitary gland. The endocrine system consists of glands such as the hypothalamus, the pituitary, and the adrenal glands. Glands communicate with each other through chemicals called hormones.

Cultural factors

Many theorists believe that pressures in Western societies are mainly responsible for the origin and maintenance of eating disorders. Society's emphasis on appearance has historically exerted much greater pressure on women than on men. Some sociological theorists believe that this double standard of attractiveness has made women overly concerned with their appearance, dieting, and body image. The idea is supported by trends in advertising that have led men to become more concerned than before about their body shape and eating habits. This seems to correlate to an increase in the number of men who now appear at clinics with eating disorders.

Sociological
Concerning human society, its structure, and how it functions.

Correlate
To have a connection in which one thing affects or depends on another.

Family theories

About half of the families of people with eating disorders have a history of making a big issue of thinness, food, and body image. Anorexia is prevalent in middle-class female children from families with high aspirations whose parents have a professional background. It is also more common in those who go on to higher education than in those who leave school at the earliest opportunity. Anorexia sufferers often strive for perfection in all they do, including the way they look. The pressure on these young women to succeed might be too great, so it sends them into a spiral of anorexia or bulimia and anxiety or depression.

Other possible causes

Cognitive-behavioral and psychodynamic theories are derived from the idea that eating disorders are linked with dieting behavior. Anorexics might be striving for perfection and so go on diets to achieve their ideal weight. When they reach this goal, they might well receive admiration from those around them, and this further reinforces their dieting behavior, which goes on in a vicious circle. Reward for not eating might come in the form of attention from family and friends. There might also be approval: the anorexic is admired for looking like an athlete or a supermodel. For bulimia sufferers, the reinforcement might come from the act of bingeing and purging, which reduces their anxious thoughts.

Substance abuse and addiction

Substance abuse refers to the regular use of a substance that causes problems in a person's day-to-day functioning. It is considered a mental disorder because it affects mood, thoughts, and behavior. There are also certain activities, such as gambling, in which people take part for stimulation. The uncontrollable or excessive use of substances and the participation in such activities are sometimes called addictions.

Curriculum Context

Students may wish to evaluate the various theories of causes of eating disorders.

Substance dependency is a repetitive action. Dependency is usually indicated when the substance becomes the central factor in people's thoughts, emotions, and actions. They are usually unsuccessful in their attempts to stop substance abuse on their own. Dependency on a substance is often indicated when tolerance and withdrawal effects are present. Tolerance is the need for increasing quantities of a substance in order to achieve the same effects as were felt before. Withdrawal symptoms include the negative physical and psychological effects that occur when a particular substance is stopped suddenly.

Prevalence

The highest levels of substance abuse are reported for people under the age of 45. This is thought to be mainly because of the social activities in which they participate, such as going to bars and clubs, and the greater availability of substances in such places.

Research also shows higher rates of alcoholism, nicotine use, and other forms of substance abuse in identical twins than in nonidentical twins. This indicates a possibility that substance abuse can be passed through families. Children of alcoholics also tend to have higher rates of excessive alcohol consumption in later life, even when they have been adopted by nondrinking parents.

Development

Peer pressure is frequently a factor in the development and continuation of substance abuse. Cigarettes and alcohol are the substances that people most commonly start to use through pressure from their social group. Media exposure might play a role in promoting

Many addictive substances are legal, including nicotine (which occurs in tobacco), caffeine (found in tea and coffee), and alcohol. Others are illegal, such as the marijuana joint this man is smoking. People might be diagnosed with substance abuse disorder only if their habit interferes with their normal functioning.

Curriculum Context

It is important to be aware of how addiction begins and is maintained.

substance use. A person is also four times more likely to develop a substance abuse problem if a family member has a similar type of dependency than if no family members have a history of addiction. Children and adolescents are more likely to abuse substances if their parents use drugs or accept drug use.

Psychological theories

Alcohol and drugs alter a person's physical and emotional experiences. In some cases they provide people with pleasure, and in others they help people avoid negative or stressful experiences. Therefore, it has been suggested that these substances reinforce addiction because they succeed in reducing stress.

Alcoholism

Alcohol is the potentially addictive substance that is most frequently used. Alcohol contains the drug ethanol, which passes directly into the bloodstream when consumed and alters the person's mental and physical functioning. Alcoholics typically lose contact with their family and friends and can develop major financial problems, medical problems, and sometimes legal problems, such as drunk-driving convictions.

Gambling can become an addiction for some people. Problem gambling can disrupt people's lives. It is likely to bring financial and social problems into the lives of those who are addicted as well as those close to them.

Drugs

Cannabis can be smoked, chewed, or eaten and is used to create feelings of relaxation and pleasure. Negative

effects of regular use include poor memory, reduced powers of concentration, increased risk of lung cancer, loss of energy, and poor motivation. Heavy use can result in anxiety, paranoia, and hallucinations.

Stimulants include cocaine and amphetamines. They are often used to increase arousal levels, confidence, and enjoyment. Negative effects of regular use include confusion, agitation, paranoia, physical disturbances such as dizziness, and sleep disruption. Many young people use stimulant or hallucinogenic drugs at clubs, bars, and all-night dance parties.

Sedatives include opium and heroin. They are generally used to reduce arousal levels and pain. Negative effects of regular use include poor coordination, confusion, and sleepiness. Sedatives are highly addictive, and withdrawal often results in negative effects, including vomiting, sleep disturbance, muscle cramps, and pain.

Nicotine is the addictive substance in tobacco. Smoking reduces stress or anxiety. Negative effects of regular use include increased risk of heart disease and cancer. Withdrawal effects include depression, disturbed sleep, anxiety, anger, and restlessness.

Dementia

Dementia is a term that generally refers to an inability to learn new information or to remember past events. It often results in a loss of reasoning ability or judgment and a general deterioration of intellectual abilities. People affected by dementia eventually become unable to perform their normal social and occupational roles.

There are many types of dementia, which differ according to their underlying cause; however, all dementias typically have several characteristics in common. Loss of memory is the most common symptom. This typically begins in a mild form but gets

> **Stimulants**
> Substances that raise levels of physiological or nervous activity in the body.

> **Sedatives**
> Drugs taken for their calming or sleep-inducing effect.

progressively worse with time. In its later stages, dementia can cause people to forget information about themselves, their location, or the time and date.

Development

People affected by dementia show poor attention and concentration. Language difficulties with dementia typically include aphasia. As the disease progresses, sufferers lose the ability to recognize their impairments. Dementia sufferers can develop changes in personality. They might become withdrawn, hostile, or lose concern for others. Some people affected with dementia are also affected by delusions. It appears that generally about 5 percent of people above the age of 65 have or will develop severe dementia. This figure rises to around 20 percent for people over the age of 80.

Alzheimer's disease

Dementia of the Alzheimer's type (DAT) was first described in 1907 by Alois Alzheimer (1864–1915). It can be formally diagnosed as Alzheimer's only after death, when an examination of the brain reveals loss of nerve cells and atrophy. Senile plaques are found throughout the brain. They are typically located near areas of the brain known to control memory and higher cognitive processes, such as self-awareness, problem solving, and reasoning abilities. DAT is progressive, degenerative, irreversible, and inevitably fatal. It typically sets in between 65 and 70 years of age. The average number of years people live following a suggested diagnosis is usually between 5 and 10 years.

Causes of DAT

Some researchers suggest there are two types of DAT: familial, which is believed to be relatively rare (1 case in 10), and sporadic, which is thought to be responsible for between 60 and 95 percent of cases. Familial Alzheimer's is believed to be genetically based. It

Aphasia
Problems of comprehension and expression.

Atrophy
The wasting away or shrinkage of brain tissue.

Senile plaques
Areas of nerve-cell loss and waxy deposits termed amyloids.

Gender-Identity Disorders

Gender-identity disorders affect how people feel about their gender. It can be very difficult to diagnose a sexual or gender-identity disorder. If you like getting dressed up as a member of the opposite sex, or cross-dressing, for example, it does not mean that you have a gender-identity disorder. These disorders are only diagnosed when people's behaviors are causing them distress or are preventing them from functioning.

The main gender-identity disorder is transsexualism, or simply gender-identity disorder. A person with this disorder feels long-term discomfort with his or her gender, referred to as gender dysphoria. They might feel disgusted by their sexual organs and strongly believe that they are supposed to be, or really are, a member of the opposite sex. A person might be preoccupied with removing the traits of their physical sex, such as facial hair in a man or a high voice in a woman. This desire might involve surgery, hormone therapy, or other medical

Transvestites are relatively common around the world, and only in a minority is cross-dressing a sign of a gender-identity disorder. Many are happy with their gender identity, and appearing as a member of the opposite sex can be a positive, or adaptive, thing for them to do.

procedures. There is a high risk of suicide and depression as people struggle with their sense of identity and dissatisfaction.

Treatment generally involves counseling, but at times gender reassignment is recommended, involving both surgery and hormone therapy. With the development of successful surgical techniques and hormone therapy, several thousand transsexuals, male and female, have undergone a permanent sex change.

occurs more commonly in people who develop dementia before the age of 60. Sporadic Alzheimer's has a late onset and no strong genetic basis.

Research tends to show that certain neurotransmitters occur in higher or lower levels than normal during dementia. For example, acetylcholine is underactive in people affected by DAT. Acetylcholine contributes to the effective functioning of movement, attention, arousal, and memory functions. Medications that block acetylcholine pathways produce symptoms similar to those found in people affected by DAT, so changes in levels of this chemical messenger might be involved in the development or continuation of the disease.

Research has linked environmental toxins to the development of DAT. Autopsies on some DAT sufferers have revealed that their brains contain high levels of aluminum. Other research has found a high rate of DAT in people with a history of head injuries.

Other dementias

Vascular dementias generally occur when blood vessels in the brain become blocked or damaged, causing a lack of oxygen and nutrients in these areas. Typical indicators include emotional ups and downs, inappropriate behavior, and changes in cognitive functioning, such as increased memory difficulties.

Subcortical dementias are degenerative disorders affecting the basal ganglia, the thalamus, and deep white matter—parts of the brain that are located under the cortex and are involved with movement. Subcortical dementias include Parkinson's disease and Huntington's chorea.

Parkinson's disease is characterized by motor (movement) problems, including resting tremor (shaking hand when at rest), muscular stiffness, and difficulty starting a particular movement. Scientists estimate that 20 to 30 percent of people with Parkinson's disease suffer from dementia. The condition primarily affects memory and executive functions, such as problem solving, judgment, and reasoning.

Autopsies
Examinations of dead bodies to discover the cause of death or the extent of disease.

Cortex
The outer layer of the brain that is concerned with consciousness.

Huntington's chorea is characterized by significant motor abnormalities, such as writhing, dancelike movements. The dementia that occurs generally results in slowed physical movement. Patients tend not to lose their memory until later stages of the disease.

Pick's disease is an extremely rare form of dementia similar to Alzheimer's. Damage to the frontal lobes of the brain is caused by loss of nerve cells and the development of Pick's bodies (a type of degraded protein). Frontal lobe dementia is caused by the deterioration of frontal lobe functioning, but there are no Pick's bodies in the brain.

Around 15 percent of people infected by the human immunodeficiency virus (HIV) develop dementia. In people with acquired immune deficiency syndrome (AIDS), the rate increases to roughly 75 percent.

Delirium

Delirium is a common disorder that causes disruption in consciousness, or awareness, and cognitive deterioration. Delirious people change in mood, behavior, and worldview. They might become agitated and try to hit out at other people or objects because they might think they are being harmed by them.

Symptoms

People affected by delirium might not recall where they are or the time or date. Their short-term memory might be affected, and they will not be able to make simple judgments correctly. Their language abilities might also be affected, so they might not understand instructions or be able to communicate clearly. They typically have severe problems when trying to write.

Sufferers from delirium might have an increased level of alertness and arousal. They might also complain of nausea, a racing heartbeat, and excessive sweating.

Curriculum Context

Students should be able to describe the symptoms and causes of the main types of dementia.

HIV
A virus that inserts its own genetic material into its hosts cells and which causes AIDS.

AIDS
A disease in which there is a severe loss of the body's cellular immunity.

They might be restless, highly talkative, and easily distracted by either internal stimuli, for example, visual disturbances such as hallucinations, or external stimuli, for example, the noise of a hospital ward. On the other hand, delirium can cause some people to have reduced levels of alertness. These people tend to lack energy and look tired and dazed, and they are often unable to follow conversations.

Delirium can also cause cycles of mood changes. For example, sufferers might feel anger or frustration at one moment, but extreme fear or confusion the next. People with delirium might become paranoid, convincing themselves that nurses are trying to harm them when they are trying to give them medication. Around half of patients experience hallucinations.

People suffering from delirium might sleep during the day and become active during the night. "Sundowning" is the term used to refer to a significant increase in the symptoms as the person is about to go to bed. It might be due to the changes in natural light as night falls.

Causes

Delirium is usually thought to arise as a result of a combination of factors. It may occur after sustaining a concussion or more severe head injury. It can also be caused by a range of medical illnesses and medications. It frequently occurs in those recovering from operations.

Scientists think that the neurotransmitter acetylcholine is involved in bringing on or maintaining delirium because levels of the neurotransmitter activity have been found to be low in people with delirium.

Alcohol, poisons, drugs, and some psychiatric medications can cause delirium. It can also develop following the withdrawal of alcohol or certain medications. It is often characterized by motor tremors, such as trembling hands. A severe form, known as delirium tremens, might develop following alcohol withdrawal. It is a dangerous and often fatal form of delirium if it is not identified and treated.

Urinary tract infections, bacterial meningitis, influenza, AIDS, and diseases of the liver, kidney, lungs, or heart can lead to delirium. Delirium can also occur following allergic reactions to food, heat stroke, electrocution, and malnutrition.

From 10 to 40 percent of hospital patients are estimated to have experienced delirium during their hospital stay, especially following an operation, due to the stress of surgery, postoperative pain, the medication given after the surgery, and infections.

Meningitis
Inflammation of the meninges, which are membranes that line the skull and enclose the brain.

Heat stroke
Excessive exposure to the sun and high temperatures.

Factitious Disorders

Both factitious and somatoform disorders can be characterized by symptoms that have no physical cause. People suffering from a factitious disorder will deliberately and voluntarily try to convince others that they are afflicted with a physical or a psychological ailment. They will intentionally fake symptoms and even inflict harm on themselves to produce the symptoms of a disease or evidence of a supposedly accidental injury. A patient might heat up a thermometer to fake a fever, for example, take drugs to induce vomiting, or throw themselves down a flight of stairs.

Despite the intent, such people are in fact suffering from a real psychological disorder. The motivating factor is the desire to assume the role of a sick person, which brings social rewards in the nature of attention from and improved relationships with other family members, friends, and medical professionals. Sufferers of factitious disorders know that they are not sick. Treatment generally involves trying to address the underlying conflicts that have lead to the disorder.

The most severe and long-term factitious disorder is commonly referred to as Münchausen's syndrome. In Münchausen's syndrome, patients can inflict severe harm on themselves. This form is more common in men than women. Some people suffer from Münchausen's by proxy, in which they inflict harm on others in their immediate care, again to seek attention. Although rare, there have been highly publicized cases of parents inflicting harm on their children as part of this disorder.

Abnormality in Development

It is likely that you are able to read this book yourself and that you are able to chat to your friends about it. However, many children grow up with psychological difficulties that affect their everyday functioning and their ability to learn.

Adolescence
The period following the onset of puberty during which a child becomes an adult.

Cognition
The processing of information by the brain.

Motor skills
The ability to control the muscles well.

Certain mental disorders are usually first diagnosed in infancy, childhood, or adolescence. These disorders are often known as abnormalities in development, and they may be further grouped as learning difficulties or emotional and behavioral disorders. Learning difficulties involve disturbances in cognition, language and speech, and academic and motor skills. In emotional and behavioral disorders, cognition is not affected. However, there is often an overlap: Learning disabilities might involve associated emotional problems, while emotional and behavioral problems often interfere with learning.

What are learning difficulties?
In 1963 a number of parents and educators of children with learning problems held a meeting in Chicago. At that time there was no agreed term used to describe such children, so the meeting agreed on the term "learning disabilities," and the Learning Disabilities Association was formed. Children with learning difficulties have the potential to learn more, but have psychological problems that restrict them doing so.

There is no universally agreed definition of learning difficulties because there is such great variation in characteristics from person to person. To identify learning difficulties, psychologists measure the difference between the potential ability and the actual achievement of the child. Potential is measured with IQ tests and other tests of ability. A learning difficulty might be diagnosed if there is a significant gap between potential and achievement.

IQ
Intelligence quotient; a number representing someone's intelligence, as measured using problem-solving tests.

The term "learning difficulties" covers a wide range of problems. Some of these problems are recognized by characteristic features or symptoms. Manuals such as the *Diagnostic and Statistical Manual* (DSM) list learning difficulties under developmental disorders and provide defining features.

Curriculum Context

Students should be familiar with the symptoms of the major learning disorders listed in the DSM.

Education

An important concern with learning difficulties is where the child should be educated or treated. Children with severe learning difficulties will usually need intensive, one-to-one teaching by special teachers. Children with milder difficulties are more likely to benefit from being in a regular classroom with a little extra help. How families cope at home is also a factor, especially when it has to be decided whether or not to place children in residential facilities. Important aims should be to educate the child in the least restrictive environment possible. The overall aim is for children's learning difficulties and behavior to improve to the point where they can be placed in a general education class.

Autism

Autism affects many areas of a person's life. Because it involves multiple symptoms, autism is often considered to be a group of disorders rather than a single disorder. It is usually apparent in a child before the age of three and affects around 5 in every 10,000 of the population. Three times as many boys as girls have autism.

Autism and social interaction

Some people with autism do not speak at all. Others have the basic skill and can name objects and actions, but are unable to describe emotions or ask questions. People with autism often appear absorbed in their own world, not even seeming to notice that others are present. Some children with autism do not mind if other people try to interact with them, while others find it completely distressing.

People with autism often are unable to grasp gestures, tone of voice, or facial expression. They find conversation difficult and often behave oddly, avoiding eye contact. They might not speak at all, speak too little, or speak all of the time, without listening to the other person. They do not recognize that in conversation people take turns in speaking and they might also make inappropriate comments. A common feature of the speech of people with autism is echolalia, which means repetition. It might be the repetition of a question before it is answered, or the repeated use of favorite words and phrases.

Curriculum Context

Students should be able to describe the range of social disabilities of children with autism.

There is a theory that people with autism are unable to analyze their own thoughts and recognize that other people have different thoughts than they do. This helps explain the difficulty that people with autism have in recognizing meaning and emotion in speech, as well as their other deficits in social interaction.

Autism and behavioral problems

People with autism often repeat actions excessively or display a persistent preoccupation with an object, idea, or feeling. Sometimes the actions are obsessive movements, such as body rocking, hand flapping, or blinking. A child with autism might run faucets constantly or insist on listening to the same song over and over. He or she might be obsessed with certain foods. Another obsession is routine. A child with autism might even find a variation in the route to school extremely distressing.

Curriculum Context

Students should consider the possible causes of behavioral problems in autistic children.

Eating, drinking, and sleeping patterns are often disrupted. People with autism will sometimes have a temper tantrum or be aggressive toward themselves or others if, for example, their routine is changed or if

somebody tries to interact with them. This is often because they panic in these situations, and because they do not understand society's rules about disruptive behavior. Children with autism frequently do not have self-care skills and lack toilet training.

Autism and intelligence

About 80 percent of sufferers score lower than 70 on IQ tests (the average score is between 85 and 115). People with autism score best on the parts of the tests measuring visual–spatial skills (such as drawing, painting, and sorting), math, and memory. In fact, people with autism often have very good memories. They score lower in parts of the tests measuring language, abstract thinking, and logic.

Possible contributing factors

Most psychologists now believe that the causes of autism are biological, but there are still disagreements over exactly how it is caused.

A child with autism receives one-to-one supervision from a special teacher. Children with learning difficulties require more intensive and often more specialized training than regular pupils of the same age.

The Wild Boy of Aveyron

In 1800 Jean-Marc-Gaspard Itard, chief medical officer of the Institute for the Deaf and Dumb in Paris, France, was introduced to a young boy, aged about 13, who had been found living in the forest in Aveyron in southern France. Nobody knew his name, so he was called the Wild Boy of Aveyron. He did not speak, avoided contact with people, rocked back and forth, and took little notice of his surroundings. He was diagnosed with congenital inborn idiocy and declared untreatable. Itard disagreed; he named the boy Victor and set about educating him. Although Victor learned very little speech, Itard taught him to read and write, and the boy's understanding and emotions developed.

Chromosome
A threadlike structure, consisting of DNA and proteins, found in the nucleus of cells.

Studies of twins have shown that there might be a genetic influence on autism. Researchers have found that if one twin has autism, it is more likely that the other will also have autism if they are identical rather than nonidentical twins. The brothers or sisters of someone with autism have a 50 times greater chance of having autism themselves than others in the general population. Other genetic researchers claim that autism is associated with "fragile-X syndrome," an abnormality in the X chromosome with symptoms very similar to those of autism. As with autism, the syndrome affects more males than females. This is because males only have one copy of the X chromosome, so if a section of the chromosome is faulty, there is no chance that a working copy occurs on the companion chromosome.

In 1977 Susan Folstein and Michael Rutter found that, if one of a pair of twins had autism, it was most likely to be the one that had experienced most problems during pregnancy or birth. However, although there seems to be some association between birth complications and autism, the exact link is still not clear.

Many scientific studies that have looked for a link between brain abnormalities and autism have provided conflicting evidence. Some scientists suggest that the findings are associated with the reticular activating system, which controls arousal and attention.

A few postmortem brain examinations have also suggested an association between abnormalities in the cerebellum and autism. The cerebellum is the large, projecting rear part of the brain that is concerned with the coordination of muscles—controlling movement, balance, and posture—and the maintenance of the body's equilibrium. A number of studies of CT (computed tomography) scans, which use X-rays, have also identified unusual features in the cerebellums of autistic people, as have some MRI (magnetic resonance imaging) studies. However, both CT and MRI data have also suggested abnormalities in various other parts of autistic people's brains. Brain abnormalities in people with autism are not common and appear to vary, so features of the brain associated with autism are difficult to identify.

Curriculum Context

Students may wish to examine the findings of brain scanning studies in relation to autism.

Researchers have collected evidence that certain foods might make autistic symptoms worse or even trigger autism. They claim that sensitivity to the proteins gluten (in wheat, rye, oats, and barley) and casein (in milk and other dairy products) are responsible for this. The theory is that people with autism are not able to break down these foods properly, leading to an excess of chemicals (peptides) that build up in the central nervous system and affect behavior, moods, and cognitive ability. Some parents report that removing gluten from the diet can reduce autistic symptoms.

Peptides

Compounds consisting of two or more amino acids.

Treatment with applied behavior analysis

Applied behavior analysis (ABA) focuses on relationships between behavior and events in the environment. Behavior analysts focus on behavioral excesses and deficits. A behavioral excess is something a person does too often; examples in autism are

throwing tantrums or causing self-injury. A behavioral deficit is something a person does too rarely, such as social interaction or speech. ABA aims to change behavior so that these excesses and deficits are reduced or even removed completely.

The first step with the ABA approach is to identify the behavior to be changed, which is termed "target behavior." It has to be precisely defined, because it is important that the behavior can be measured and recorded. The next step is to record the behavior before the intervention begins. This is so that a before-and-after picture can be built up showing whether the intervention has been successful.

Grandmother and child work together to build a jigsaw puzzle. Her praise, when he succeeds, encourages him and serves as a reinforcer for his behavior. Applied behavior analysis (ABA) treats children with autism with similar social reinforcers. Behavior analysts train parents and other family members to use ABA techniques, both in courses and during home visits.

The next step is to look for relationships between the target behavior and events in the environment and then change the environment to change the behavior. For example, it is often found that tantrums are reinforced by social attention. In this case, the change in the environment that might reduce tantrums would be to avoid giving attention during a tantrum. Removing reinforcement is called extinction. It is also important to give attention when no tantrum is happening, which teaches the child to behave calmly.

Shaping

A common method of teaching new skills to a child with autism is called shaping. It involves teaching a skill in small steps. For example, in teaching speech to a child who has never spoken, the therapist initially reinforces every sound. Only when the child is making sounds regularly will the therapist begin to reinforce syllables (or parts of words). The therapist gradually increases the complexity of speech to build up the learning of meaningful language. Therapists also use antecedent events in teaching skills. For example, in the presence of a red object the therapist might say, "That is colored red. Say red." The antecedents are the colored object and the therapist's instruction. If the child responds correctly, the behavior will then be reinforced.

ABA has often been found to be effective in changing the behavior of people with autism and in teaching them new skills. The earlier in a child's life treatment begins, the more likely it is to be successful. It also requires intensive one-to-one contact with the therapist over a long period of time. Programs have been set up to train parents to be therapists for their own children. In this way, children are more likely to receive the maximum possible amount of treatment.

The TEACCH program

TEACCH stands for Treatment and Education of Autistic and related Communication–handicapped Children. The program was founded to teach communication and understanding of social meaning. The key elements are classroom structure and organization.

It is important to organize the classroom in a way that will help the student with autism learn. The setup should not be changed, because people with autism do not like change. Distractions are kept to a minimum, which can be done by covering windows, for example. Different tasks are assigned to different areas of the classroom, with the relevant materials for these tasks kept conveniently nearby. This helps the child with autism understand what tasks should be done where.

Schedules help make the school day more predictable and reduce the stress that unexpected events can cause. Usually there is a schedule for the whole class

Antecedent
Relating to something that existed before or logically preceeds another.

Curriculum Context

Many curricula expect students to be aware of the ways in which autistic children can be taught successfully.

that breaks the day up into sessions, while each child also has an individual schedule of what he or she should be doing in each session. At the end of each activity the teacher provides a reinforcer, such as money, praise, a snack, or a favorite activity, before moving on to the next activity. This motivates the student to work right through a session. The setting up of joint activities that the student enjoys and that involve learning skills encourages the student to communicate.

Savant syndrome

The term "savant syndrome" refers to people with developmental disabilities who are skilled in one or more areas. Only about half of savants have autism, with the other half exhibiting various other disabilities. The level of skill varies. A rare minority (probably fewer than a hundred in the whole world) are classified as prodigious savants. In such cases, the level of skill is far beyond that which could be expected from someone in the general population. Sometimes the skills are so extreme, and present without having been learned, that they are difficult to believe.

Dyslexia

The term "dyslexia" usually refers to problems in reading. It involves difficulty in recognizing words and interpreting written or printed information. People with dyslexia might also have difficulties in reading other symbols, such as written music. The reading of numerals can also be affected, causing problems with math. This is termed dyscalculia. If people with dyslexia are able to read at all, they generally read slowly, hesitantly, and inaccurately.

People with dyslexia often have difficulty writing as well. The trouble is usually associated with reading problems, but might occur on its own. The technical term for this is dysgraphia. It involves difficulty in

Curriculum Context

Students may wish to examine the theories linking mental impairment in one or more fields with extreme skills in specific areas.

Inspirations for Rain Man

In the 1988 movie *Rain Man,* Dustin Hoffman plays an autistic savant. To prepare for the movie, he spent time with a number of savants, including Joseph Sullivan and Kim Peek, and partly based his character on them.

Joseph Sullivan has great mental arithmetical skill. He is also skilled at memorizing numbers and can read and memorize encyclopedias. Sullivan also has a number of rituals, such as eating cheeseballs with a toothpick, a mannerism that Hoffman used in the movie.

Kim Peek was also mathematically gifted, but his main skills were in reading and memory. Before he was two years old, he could memorize any book read to him. He read and memorized more than 7,500 books. He read each book only once. Peek was not behaviorally autistic: he had a warm and affectionate nature. Known as Kimputer, he was a walking encyclopedia on several subjects, including literature, zip and telephone area codes, sports statistics, history, highway routes, and classical music.

forming words and writing in a straight line. People with dyslexia often spell words in an unusual manner, write the letters in the wrong order, or confuse letters.

Prevalence of dyslexia

Estimates suggest that about 10 percent of the population are dyslexic to some degree, with about 4 percent being severely dyslexic. Dyslexia is a condition that is present from birth. Without special education, the problems associated with it continue throughout a person's life and make everyday tasks very difficult.

Other problems associated with dyslexia are a confused sense of space and difficulty in following directions, a poor sense of time, bad organization, and bad short-term memory. People with dyslexia are generally of average or above average intelligence, and are often skilled in other fields.

Dyslexia can lead to emotional problems such as distress, frustration, and a fear of reading and writing, especially if the dyslexia has not been recognized, and the person does not understand what is wrong. Many

Curriculum Context

Students may find it useful to list the ways in which an inability to read affects daily life.

children go through school and into adulthood with the condition unrecognized.

Phonology

Phonology is concerned with the individual elements from which words are constructed. Even short words are made up of a number of smaller units or sounds, called phonemes. When we speak, we automatically, and very quickly, put these units together to make words. When we read, we perceive marks on a page (letters) with our eyes and brain, and mentally convert them into phonemes before they come together as words. Many researchers have found that a lack of ability to break words down into phonemes coincides with dyslexia.

Genetics and dyslexia

A number of studies have found that dyslexia tends to run in families. This does not prove a genetic influence, though, since characteristics may pass through families because of environmental influences. Twin studies have found that twins can be similarly affected by dyslexia and associated conditions. Identical twins have exactly the same genes, while nonidentical twins have different sets of genes. If both members of a pair of identical twins have reading problems more often than both members of a pair of nonidentical twins, we can assume that the difference is because of a genetic influence. In 1985 Sadie Decker and Bruce Bender carried out just such a study. They found that 85 percent of the identical pairs were both dyslexic, while 55 percent of the nonidentical pairs were both dyslexic.

Brain structure and dyslexia

One area of the brain that has been linked with dyslexia is the planum temporale. There are two plana temporale, one in each hemisphere, and they are located in areas that deal with language. For most people, the one on the left side is larger than the one

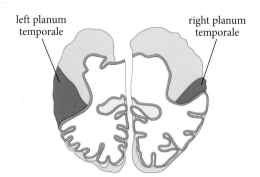

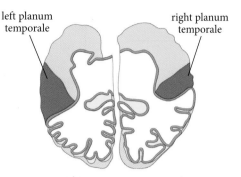

Brain of normal person   Brain of person with dyslexia

The left planum temporale in the brain of a normal person is larger than that on the right. In a dyslexic person's brain both are the same size. It is not known what the function of the plana temporale is because it is difficult to test them, since they are buried deep within the brain. The left planum temporale, however, is situated near the language cortex. (In both these diagrams the cross section shows both plana temporale partially covered by other brain structures.)

on the right. However, when Dr. Albert Galaburda carried out postmortem examinations, he found that in dyslexics this area is often the same size on both sides. The left-hand side is the same size as normal but the right-hand side is larger than usual, making the two sides symmetrical. This has also been found in MRI studies, so the relationship between symmetrical plana temporale and dyslexia seems clear. We do not know how this affects reading, but the fact that one of the plana temporale is in the area of the brain associated with language links with the phonological model.

Postmortem examinations have found that small wartlike clusters of brain cells, called ectopias, are common in dyslexics. Studies with mice show that ectopias are associated with difficulty in learning tasks.

Research has also found that there are differences in the thalamus, an area of the brain that is part of our sensory system. In dyslexics, the cells in the thalamus that deal with visual information are smaller than usual. This can affect eye movements, spatial skills, and visual attention. The cells in the part of the thalamus

Postmortem

An examination of a dead body to establish the cause of death.

dealing with sound information are also smaller, and this might be linked to the phonological problems.

Teaching methods

The overall aim of treating dyslexia is to increase the fluency of reading and writing. Most teaching uses a phonetic approach, which concentrates on sounds. The main problem in dyslexia is relating sounds to letters and groups of letters, so the general aim of teaching is to establish these connections.

The Alpha to Omega method

Alpha to Omega is an effective method for treating dyslexia. It involves structured step-by-step teaching, building up from simple reading skills to complex skills. The first step is to teach associations between single letters and sounds. Students are shown a card with a letter on one side and a picture on the other. The teacher shows the picture and names it "apple," for example, then turns over the card and reads the letter "A." The students repeat these sounds and also copy the letters and read them out loud. This continues until they have learned all of the letters and can read them by themselves, and can write them when the teacher

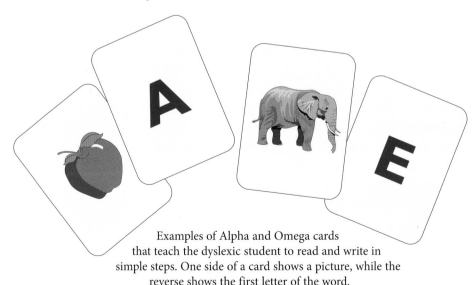

Examples of Alpha and Omega cards
that teach the dyslexic student to read and write in
simple steps. One side of a card shows a picture, while the
reverse shows the first letter of the word.

dictates them. When the students have learned single letters, the process is repeated with phonemes (sounds) made up of more than one letter, such as "th" and "sh." As students learn phonemes and rules, they apply the skills to sentence construction. First, the teacher says a sentence, which students repeat. Then the teacher slowly says the sentence again, while the students write it down. They then read aloud what they have written. Finally, the teacher helps them correct any reading and writing errors. It is important that these sentences only include phonemes and rules that the students have used so far. It is also important that the sentence is understandable, relevant, and interesting to the students. As their skills improve, they can learn more complex sentences.

Curriculum Context

Students should be able to explain the current approaches to helping children with dyslexia to read.

The Fernald method

The Fernald method is used in cases in which phonetic methods have been unsuccessful. It teaches students to read whole words and involves the use of vision, sound, movement, and touch. The students choose which word they want to learn, and the teacher writes it down in large letters. The teacher reads it, and the students repeat it. The students then trace over the written word with their finger, pronouncing it as they go. Sometimes the letters are cut out of materials with an interesting texture.

Colored overlays, lenses, and lamps

Researchers have found that for some people who have dyslexia, printed text seems to move around on the page. Colored transparent plastic overlays placed over the page can reduce this problem and improve reading. Colored lenses in glasses or colored lamps shining on the page can also help.

Treating dysgraphia

Dysgraphia describes the handwriting problems often associated with dyslexia. Students can learn many strategies to overcome dysgraphia. Most involve repeated practice aimed at increasing the quality, accuracy, and speed of writing. Some of these strategies are copying and tracing words and filling in missing letters in words to improve spelling. It is, of course, important that the students have already learned to read the words they are learning to spell, so what they are writing has meaning to them. In one method, students first study a written word, then cover it and attempt to write it. Finally, they uncover the example, compare it with what they have written, and describe any differences.

ADHD

Attention deficit hyperactivity disorder (ADHD) is the most common reason for children to be referred to psychiatrists and psychologists. It is estimated that between 4 and 6 percent of people in the United States have ADHD, and doctors are increasingly diagnosing more with the disorder. About three-quarters of people with the disorder are male. About half of those diagnosed with ADHD in childhood still have the symptoms when they become adults. For a diagnosis of ADHD, six of the symptoms (*see* box on page 61) should be present for at least six months and should be considered to be inappropriate for a child of that age.

Symptoms of ADHD

Children with ADHD find it difficult to concentrate for long periods of time. The problem of inattention is usually worse in the afternoon and evening than it is in the morning. Inattention also applies to activities outside school. ADHD children finish their meals after everybody else because they do not concentrate on eating. They find it difficult to have long conversations, and they often change from one activity to another. Inattention does not apply to all activities, though. Children with ADHD will often have a few favorite activities on which they concentrate even more than

Hyperactivity

Abnormal or extreme activity.

Curriculum Context

Students might consider the individual symptoms of ADHD and explain how each symptom hinders learning.

other children do. They often sleep less than other children, going to bed late and getting up early.

ADHD children are often impulsive. This is considered by many as being the most important symptom in diagnosing the condition. Children with ADHD seem to act without thinking. Because they do not plan their actions, they appear to be disorganized and make mistakes. They are not good at following rules because they do not think about them before they act. Impatience can lead to frustration when they do not quickly get what they want.

Associated problems

The impulsivity of children with ADHD can be dangerous since they often have poor road-safety skills and take part in dangerous activities. Children with ADHD have difficulty in learning because they are easily distracted and have trouble concentrating. They might miss part of what the teacher is talking about, not read all of the information they are required to, and not complete assignments. They then fall behind in their schoolwork and find it very difficult to catch up. Children with ADHD often have very untidy handwriting because they tend to rush everything they do. ADHD can have an extreme effect on academic performance, with children with ADHD being far more

Main Features of ADHD

Inattention
- does not pay attention to details or makes careless mistakes
- has difficulty paying attention to tasks and activities
- does not seem to listen when spoken to
- does not follow instructions and fails to complete tasks
- has difficulty organizing tasks and activities
- avoids tasks that require concentration
- often loses things
- is easily distracted
- is often forgetful

Hyperactivity
- often fidgets or squirms in seat
- often leaves seat when sitting is expected
- often runs around or climbs excessively in inappropriate situations
- has difficulty playing or carrying out activities quietly
- often seems very energetic
- often talks excessively

Impulsivity
- often shouts out answers before questions have been completed
- often has difficulty waiting turn
- often interrupts conversations or games

(Summarized from the DSM)

likely than their peers to drop out of school early and less likely to go on to a college education. Psychologists think that ADHD children are probably of normal intelligence. It is difficult to measure the IQ of these children, because they have great trouble in concentrating on the tests.

Children with ADHD find it difficult to make friends. That is because they are unable to concentrate and become easily bored during conversations and will often butt in. They are also poor at taking turns in games. Also, their hyperactive and impulsive behavior sometimes makes other children avoid them.

Poor academic performance and difficulty in making friends can lead to people with ADHD having low self-esteem and other emotional problems. They might become frustrated and aggressive, often losing their temper easily. Some might even become delinquent, carrying out criminal acts. It is thought that this is a result of feelings that they are being excluded from society and punished for behavior they cannot control.

Attention deficit disorder

Not all children with problems of attention and impulsivity are hyperactive. The term ADD (attention deficit disorder) without hyperactivity is used to describe these children. While they experience very many of the same problems as children with full ADHD, such as learning difficulties and difficulties in making friends, they are more often not diagnosed. That is because hyperactivity is one of the more noticeable symptoms of the condition.

Possible causes

Most researchers think that the main factors that lead to the development of ADHD are biological. MRI studies have found differences in several parts of the brains of ADHD children. The corpus callosum, which connects

The limbic system in the brain is involved in how we express our mood and instincts. Its main parts are the thalamus and the corpus striatum (green), which consists of the caudate nucleus and the lentiform (comma-shaped) nucleus. The caudate nucleus is smaller in people diagnosed with ADHD.

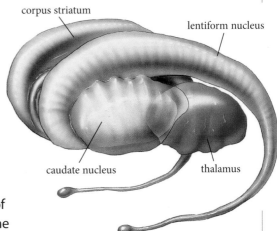

corpus striatum

lentiform nucleus

caudate nucleus

thalamus

the left-hand and right-hand halves of the brain, is smaller than usual in some children with ADHD. The corpus callosum is the pathway through which information from the two halves of the brain is integrated. The caudate nucleus is also smaller in children with ADHD. The functions of the caudate nucleus include self-control and attention. It is part of the limbic system, which is located in the forebrain and controls memory and emotions.

Research has also suggested that brain activity, rather than brain structure, might be connected to ADHD. Results have suggested that the brains of children with ADHD function slightly differently. It seems that there is less activity than normal in frontal areas of the brain, areas that help control activity, attention, and emotion.

People with ADHD have lower levels of certain neurotransmitters than normal. The symptoms of ADHD may be explained by a lack of the neurotransmitters that are involved with self-control and attention. The three main neurotransmitters thought to be affected are serotonin, dopamine, and noradrenaline. Some studies have found that children with ADHD have fewer of the waste products of noradrenaline.

The main evidence for a genetic influence on ADHD comes from twin studies. ADHD affects between approximately 4 percent and 6 percent of the population. However, if one twin has ADHD, there is

Curriculum Context

Students can usefully explore the possible biological and genetic causes of ADHD.

about a 30 percent chance that the other twin will also have the disorder. For identical twins, the probability rises to more than 75 percent.

Medical treatments

In the 1930s scientists unexpectedly discovered that amphetamine drugs can reduce hyperactivity and aggression and increase concentration and attention. This has led to psychiatrists using stimulant drugs to treat ADHD. The most commonly used drug is called Ritalin. It begins to have an effect about a half-hour after it is taken and lasts for between three and five hours, so it is generally taken three or four times a day. It works by increasing the amount of dopamine in the brain, which then reduces ADHD symptoms.

The use of drugs to treat ADHD is controversial. Many people think that children are being drugged when they just need help. There are also side effects. Sleep patterns might be disturbed and appetite reduced. Children may become tense or twitchy.

Psychological approaches

Behavior therapy techniques can be useful in treating ADHD. They are often used in the classroom and can also be used by parents. Positive behavior should be noticed and rewarded. It should also be recognized that disruptive or argumentative behavior can be accidentally rewarded by attention; it is often better to ignore such behavior. Doing this removes the positive consequence that the behavior has been getting. Punishment is generally ineffective in dealing with ADHD behavior.

Psychotherapy tackles the emotional side of ADHD. The children talk with a trained therapist about their behavior and their feelings. A greater understanding of themselves can help them develop a more positive outlook and tackle their problems.

Amphetamine

An addictive, mood-altering drug, used as a stimulant.

Curriculum Context

By examining research findings, students can compare how effective drugs, behavioral therapy, and psychotherapy are in helping people with ADHD.

Success Story

When he was a child in the 1950s, Jack D. Barchas's ambition was to be a doctor and researcher. At school, though, he had problems with reading and spelling. In second grade his teacher told his father that he was retarded. His father disagreed and took him to see Dr. Grace Fernald. At first Dr. Fernald tutored Jack in her home. After a while he enrolled in the small class in which her program was run. There was a student-teacher for every two pupils, with Dr. Fernald in charge of the class. The program worked so well for Jack that he is now Professor Jack D. Barchas, chair of psychiatry at New York Hospital Cornell Medical Center. Previous to that he was dean of neuroscience and research at UCLA. He is one of many successes, and nearly 50 years later the Grace Fernald School at UCLA is still helping young people with dyslexia.

Help for families

Developmental disabilities affect the whole family. Parents often need to spend a lot of time dealing with the child, which can be very stressful. The parents might doubt their own parenting skills and feel helpless and inadequate if their child's condition does not improve despite their efforts to solve the problem. Parents often feel guilty, angry, confused, or even resentful of their child. Counseling can help parents and other family members cope with their feelings.

One of the most important things for parents is that they feel involved in their child's treatment. Parents might simply be told of the treatment their child is receiving and be advised on how to interact with their child at home. Alternatively, parents might receive professional training so that they can provide extra therapy for the child at home. Parents often find support groups very useful. Here they come together to share their experiences of living with a child with developmental difficulties.

Curriculum Context

Students should consider the extent to which parents can help improve the quality of life for children with ADHD.

Psychotherapies

Sigmund Freud pioneered psychotherapy—or the "talking cure"— with his theory of psychoanalysis. The idea of talking to someone to relieve anxiety or distress is an age-old tradition practiced across many cultures. Nowadays many different psychotherapies are used to treat a wide range of mental disorders.

The word "psychotherapy" refers to the treatment of mental disorders by psychological means. It is the ideas behind the therapy, the way that it is applied, and the nature of the relationships that develop between the client and the therapist that differentiate between types of psychotherapy.

Psychotherapy is provided by mental-health professionals from a range of disciplines, including psychiatrists, clinical and counseling psychologists, psychotherapists, art and drama therapists, and counselors. Psychotherapies reflect the many different approaches, or perspectives, that historically people have used to study psychology.

Psychoanalysis

Psychoanalysis was the first psychodynamic theory. The term "psychodynamic" describes the root causes of behavior and the forces within the personality that motivate it. The psychodynamic model sees mental disorders as stemming from an imbalance between the id, ego, and superego, the three principal components of the personality proposed by Sigmund Freud.

The basic assumption of Freud's theory is that much of our behavior stems from processes that are unconscious. Emotionally painful feelings, memories, and wishes can become repressed, that is, diverted to the unconscious. They can reach consciousness in disguised ways, through dreams, irrational behavior, mannerisms, and slips of the tongue.

The purpose of psychoanalysis is to bring out repressed fears and motives from the unconscious into the person's consciousness so they can be dealt with in a more rational and realistic way. When people understand what is motivating them, they can deal more effectively with their problem.

Anxiety and defenses

Freud believed that most mental disorders are the result of unconscious conflicts between the aggressive and sexual impulses of the id and the constraints imposed by the ego and superego. These conflicts, repressed since childhood, prevent the person from coping in adulthood in a mature way. If the ego is too weak to cope with the demands of either the id or superego, it defends itself by repressing them into the unconscious. The greater the restraint on expression of impulses by society, the greater the conflict will be between the three parts of the personality. Defense mechanisms are never totally successful, and residual tension spills out into everyday life. All defense mechanisms involve an element of self-deception.

Freud argued that if repressed material could be dredged up and people forced to confront the crisis rather than deny it, then full recovery should follow.

Curriculum Context

Many curricula ask students to describe how the theories of psychoanalysis are put into practice in psychoanalytic therapy.

Taking part in vigorous, highly competitive sport, such as a game of squash, can be a way of diverting the impulses of the id—the primitive, unruly forces that according to Freud form part of personality.

The German-born psychoanalyst Erich Fromm began as a follower of Freud but broke away from Freud's teachings because he thought people's personalities were shaped by society as well as biological drives. In turn, he used psychoanalytic thinking to explain the nature of modern society.

Attitudes during analysis

According to Freud, during analysis the analysand shows certain attitudes that the analyst can use as the basis of the analysis. He developed the concept of resistance to address blocks in therapy on the part of the client. During free association, the client must speak freely about anything that comes to mind, without inhibition. Freud not only observed carefully what his clients said, but also when they faltered or stopped talking altogether. When clients remained silent, they were thought to be resisting the recall of certain thoughts and feelings. Freud believed that resistance results from the person's unconscious control over sensitive areas, and that these areas are precisely the ones that the therapist should explore.

Sooner or later, clients develop a strong attitude toward the analyst. The attitude might be positive and friendly or negative and hostile. Clients express attitudes that they feel toward people who are (or were) important in their life. Often these reactions are considered to be repetitions of the original feelings dredged up from the past but transferred during therapy onto the analyst. Analysts use these feelings to explain to clients the origins of their concerns.

Freud's successors

Those who came after Freud gave greater recognition to factors other than biological drives in shaping human behavior. For example, some emphasized the importance of social and cultural factors, while others emphasized spiritual and religious factors. Some placed more emphasis on the ego in directing behavior and solving problems and less emphasis on the role of unconscious drives. These followers of Freud are called ego analysts. They suggested that people were more rational in their planning and decisions than Freud had proposed, and emphasized the effect of early relationships on mental health.

Limitations

Psychoanalysis does not recognize the importance of thought in neurosis: It is less concerned with the thoughts themselves than with the hidden meaning that it claims underlies them. Freud also failed to take into account that people are products of the society in which they live. For example, his data were biased toward the clients that he saw—mainly middle-class Jewish women during the late 19th century, when sexual standards were very strict—and much of his clients' conflict centered on guilt regarding sexual desires. Today, there is less sexual guilt.

Neurosis
A mild mental illness involving symptoms of stress.

Behavior therapy

Behaviorism is concerned with observable behavior. For example, a person might feel angry and report this or exhibit angry behavior, but the behaviorist would not speculate about the person's internal mental activity or state. Today, few psychologists would regard themselves as strict behaviorists.

Curriculum Context

Students are expected to understand and describe the theories behind behavior therapy.

Behaviorism formed the basis of learning theory, or what is also known as stimulus–response (S–R) psychology. Stimulus–response psychology studies conditioning: the stimuli, or triggers, that cause responses, the rewards and punishments that maintain certain responses, and the changes in behavior that can be observed when the pattern of rewards and responses is altered.

Therapeutic methods

Behaviorists believe that people develop behavioral problems to cope with stressful situations. They think that behaviorist techniques used in experiments on learning can be applied to unlearning maladaptive behavior and learning more adaptive behavior.

Adaptive
Able to adjust to new conditions.

Sensitization is a form of learning through which a person (or animal) learns to strengthen (intensify) his reaction to a weak stimulus if it is followed by a threatening or painful stimulus. For example, we learn to respond more intensely to the sound of a piece of equipment if it is followed by a crash. Desensitization is a "deconditioning" process behaviorists employ for people who have become sensitized. Desensitization is effective for treating fears or phobias.

Behavior therapy distinguishes symbolic, or imaginal, desensitization from actual desensitization. In symbolic desensitization the client does not encounter the feared situation. By presenting milder forms of the stimulus and allowing clients slowly to accustom themselves to it, usually combined with relaxation techniques, it is possible gradually to make the stimulus like the original. Eventually, the client becomes desensitized to the stimulus, the reaction is lost, and the fear is removed.

Actual desensitization is usually more effective than symbolic desensitization. Clients are exposed to the feared situation through a series of carefully graduated steps. Only when they have managed to

A child learns through sensitization to handle a toad that he might previously have learned to fear—associating frogs (a weak response) with another (strong) response, such as an unpleasant experience. He can unlearn his fear through reversing the process, or desensitization— touching the animal without any ill effect.

tolerate each small step until the anxiety subsides do they move on to a more anxiety-provoking stage.

In the flooding technique, clients are forced right away to confront the object triggering the fear response. However, although effective with some types of phobia, the increased anxiety for some people is too much. As a result, therapists use this type of technique with extreme caution.

Another behavioral technique can be used to treat phobias. It involves weakening the established response by strengthening the opposite response. The process works on the basis that it is impossible to feel two opposite things at the same time. Therefore, one way of systematically desensitizing people is to teach them to relax first before either imagining or being shown a picture of the feared situation.

Another effective way of changing behavior is through modeling. In treatment, observing the behavior of a model has proved successful in reducing fears and teaching new skills, and studies have shown that modeling successfully treats phobias.

Curriculum Context

Students might compare the techniques of psychoanalytic and behavior therapy and their advantages and limitations.

Behavior therapy is carefully constructed so that clients are encouraged, usually without their being aware of the encouragement, to respond in a certain way. These responses are immediately reinforced and, therefore, repeated more often.

Limitations of behaviorism

Cognitive theorists have criticized behaviorism on the grounds that there is more to learning than associating a stimulus with a response. Learning cannot be understood solely through studying environmental factors. We first mentally encode external material and then operate on these mental representations rather than on actual external stimuli.

One consequence of only looking at behavioral changes is that the client can substitute one symptom for another, for example, fear of snakes for fear of heights. Punishment might extinguish one behavior, but it is likely to resurface unless substituted with a more adaptive strategy. Sometimes behavior therapy is not substantial enough even for disorders such as phobias, where it has a good success rate.

Authoritarian

Enforcing obedience to authority, at the expense of personal freedom.

Therapists play an authoritarian role. They also take control by choosing all the rewards or reinforcements for behavioral change. Insight, and therefore intellectual empowerment, is not encouraged.

Cognitive theory

Cognitive psychologists are concerned with the scientific study of mental processes. Cognitive theory states that we do not passively respond to external events but actively develop our own explanations and give meaning to the world around us. These mental reconstructions of external events have been called "mental schema."

Schema

A model or outline of a theory.

Cognitive psychologists are concerned with how we perceive, code, and categorize events. They look for how external events influence our memory so as to develop a theory that will predict our behavior. Among the main concepts are the notions of the self, the schemata, and self-constructs. The self is considered to be a system of self-concepts that organize and guide information relating to ourselves.

Schemata are theories or generalizations about the self that we gain from past experience. Evidence of schemata can be seen in automatic thoughts or behavior, or in stable cognitions, which remain the same despite external changes. When we face a particular situation, a schema related to the situation is activated. However, someone prone to depression would typically upset this orderly pattern and respond with one that is biased or overly negative.

Self-constructs are made up of how we think: They are coded as general and abstract representations of events, objects, and relationships in the real world. We become experts about our personal constructs and seek feedback that confirms our beliefs about ourselves. We also twist or distort information that does not support our self-construct. The cognitive model sees mental disorders as resulting from distortions in cognitions.

Cognitive therapy

The aim of cognitively based therapies is to show clients that their distorted or irrational thoughts mainly contribute to their difficulties. Cognitive therapy aims to help people choose actions that are likely to change unhelpful ways of thinking. It is not simply enough to help clients change the content of a particular thought; it is essential that they recognize and change the reasoning process that led to the false conclusion in order to avoid making similar errors in the future. Since the beliefs have usually been present from an early age, they tend to be resistant to change. There are no simple ways of highlighting these faulty

Cognitive therapy is based on cognitive theory. It is concerned with how we see ourselves and how we give meaning to the world around us. We do so through mental representations that we make of things outside ourselves, which allow us to make suppositions about them.

assumptions, but a useful start is to identify recurring stressful situations in the client's life.

In other words, cognitive therapy helps us see that there are many ways we give meaning to feelings and events and how these meanings might either make us feel better or worse. This type of therapy is primarily about changing our thoughts about ourselves, the world, and the future.

Since the end of the last century, cognitive therapy has been successfully used to help clients with depression, panic disorder, phobias, anxiety, anger, stress-related disorder, relationship problems, drug and alcohol abuse, eating disorders, and most of the other difficulties that bring people to therapy.

Rational emotive therapy

Rational emotive therapy (RET) has played a large part in cognitive therapy as we know it today. Albert Ellis (1913–2007) argued that many emotional difficulties are due to the irrational beliefs people bring to their experiences. He believed that self-consciousness maintained emotional distress. Some people had learned to fear their own self-talk. Once this was recognized, they could objectively define and analyze their own fears.

Self-consciousness
The knowledge of oneself as a conscious being.

The central theme of RET is that we are uniquely rational as well as uniquely irrational. If we learn to increase our rational thinking and decrease our irrational thinking, we can rid ourselves of most of our emotional or mental unhappiness.

Effective therapists should keep unmasking their clients' past and presenting the clients with their illogical thinking and self-defeating internal sentences. They should do this by bringing the faulty thinking forcefully to the client's attention or consciousness, showing the clients how they are maintaining or causing their unhappiness, showing clients what are illogical links in their internalized sentences, and showing clients how to rethink, challenge, contract, and reword their sentences so that their internalized thoughts become more logical and efficient.

Logical
Concerning reasoning conducted according to strict rules of validity.

Ellis agreed with psychoanalysts that most faulty thinking and beliefs were instilled by people's parents. He added that these ideas also became part of the person's core beliefs or thinking patterns because they were internalized at a time in childhood before rational thought was possible.

Cognitive behavioral therapy

Cognitive behavioral therapy (CBT) is a structured, problem-focused therapy incorporating cognitive, behavioral, and emotional change. Cognitive techniques, such as challenging negative automatic thoughts, and behavioral techniques, such as graded exposure and activity scheduling, are used to relieve symptoms by changing dysfunctional thoughts, beliefs, and behavior.

Cognitive behavioral therapy works on thinking and behavior. The behavior strategy might be to desensitize someone who is afraid of heights by going up in an elevator in gradual stages. The cognitive strategy would be to replace fear-inducing thinking with a positive outlook.

Cognitive behavioral therapy has also been widely applied to the so-called affective disorders: depression and anxiety. In addition, anxiety disorders with marked symptomatic anxiety are likely to benefit from CBT. Many research studies report its effectiveness. It has become the treatment of choice for a wide range of mental-health problems.

The behavioral part of the treatment comes into play after clients devise alternative ways of viewing their

situation, and the therapist encourages them to test these new alternatives in their daily life. The therapist uses a number of techniques to challenge negative thinking or "faulty beliefs." They include mood monitoring and diary keeping. Alternatively, behavioral techniques, such as desensitization are combined with positive self-instruction to replace self-defeating internal dialogues.

A Cognitive Therapy Self-Monitoring Sheet

By keeping a thought record during situations that cause problem behavior clients can monitor their thoughts and modify them.

Situation
Who? What? When? Where?
Sunday evening, in the airplane, on the runway, waiting for the plane to take off.

Moods
What did you feel? Rate intensity of mood 0–100%
Fear (98%)

Automatic thoughts (Images)
What was going through your mind just before you started to feel this way?
- I'm feeling sick.
- My heart is starting to beat harder and faster.
- I'm starting to sweat.
- I'm having a heart attack ("hot thought," the one that produces the most anxiety, etc.).
- I'm going to die.

Evidence that supports the "hot thought"
- My heart is racing.

- I'm sweating.
- These are two symptoms of a heart attack.

Evidence that does not support the "hot thought"
- A rapid heartbeat can be a sign of anxiety.
- My doctor told me that the heart was a muscle: using a muscle is not dangerous, and therefore a rapid heartbeat is not dangerous.
- A rapid heartbeat does not mean that I am having a heart attack.
- I have had this happen to me before in airports, on airplanes, and when thinking about flying.
- In the past my heartbeat has returned to normal when I read a magazine, practiced deep breathing, or thought in more calm ways.

Alternative/balanced thoughts
- My heart is racing, and I am sweating because I'm anxious about being on an airplane (95%).
- A rapid heartbeat is not necessarily dangerous, and in all likelihood my heartbeat will return to normal in just a few minutes (85%).

Rerate moods now
Fear (25%)

Limitations of cognitive therapies

Some people have challenged the assumption that feelings follow thoughts. Research shows that in severely depressed clients, once the depression lifts, so does the negative thinking. Therefore, a predisposition to depression because of a cognitive (thinking) style is questionable. Most psychiatrists believe that the negative thinking found in depression is a symptom rather than a cause of depression.

Cognitively based therapy works best on clients who have a clearly defined problem or diagnosis, such as generalized anxiety disorder, depression, specific phobia, or posttraumatic stress disorder. Those with less clearly defined problems or who are unable to clearly articulate their problems would not be considered suitable for cognitive-based therapy.

Other therapies

Most psychotherapists use a combination of elements from the numerous therapies that have developed since Freud's time. Some of these therapies are well established and widely used.

Gestalt therapy is based on Gestalt theory, which states that we think in terms of whole situations rather than a combination of separate elements. Existential therapy tackles major philosophical issues in the client's life, such as death, freedom, and isolation.

Feminist therapy explores gender and other social roles that contribute to the client's psychological distress. It does not cater solely to women and can also be beneficial to men. Systemic therapy seeks to influence the dynamics of various relationships. Family therapy focuses on interaction between family members. Group therapy is conducted by a qualified therapist with a group of clients. Each member of the group benefits through interaction with the others.

Transactional analysis (TA) is a psychoanalytically based group therapy. It works on three ego states (parent, child, and adult) through which we relate to others.

Art therapy uses creating or viewing art as a way to express feelings. The goal is to use the creative process to help clients with their problems. Drama therapy uses aspects of the theater to explore the client's "story." Clients can use verbal and nonverbal ways to enact their own drama, which can help them dissipate psychological tensions and understand their situation.

Dissipate
To break up and drive off.

Solution-focused therapy seeks to find effective ways in which clients can solve their problems in a fixed period of time. It can take many forms and focuses on the present rather than the past.

Humanistic therapy
In contrast to the other approaches outlined in this chapter, humanistic therapy seeks to understand people's personal perception of events without imposing any theory or preconceptions.

Humanistic theory states that to understand people, we have to see the world through their eyes. It is simply interested in a person's self-concept, feelings of self-esteem, and self-awareness. The method assumes that clients are experts on their own experience and hold the key to their own cure. Emphasis in therapy is on the therapist's genuineness, or "unconditional positive regard," a feature that is likely to have been missing in the client's upbringing.

Curriculum Context

Students should be able to describe humanistic therapy and compare it with other popular forms of psychotherapy.

Humanists believe that we have a strong motivational force, or drive, toward developing our potential. Although obstacles might stand in our way, our natural tendency is to progress beyond where we are now. Some humanists reject scientific psychology,

Overcoming the odds. Humanistic therapy believes that humans are motivated to reach their full potential. It does not try to understand people through any particular line of thinking, but seeks to view their situation through their own eyes.

claiming that its methods have little to contribute to our understanding of human nature.

Carl Rogers (1902–1987) believed that psychological problems lie in the "gap" between people's real or spontaneous self and that which they present to the world. The gap is thought to be the result of conditional love by parents in childhood. A child's need for love and acceptance is paramount, and, when unmet, leads to inner confusion and conflict. Self-criticism and perfectionism are typical outcomes of this type of upbringing, and clients are likely to feel at odds with, or unaccepting of, their real selves.

The main features of this type of therapy are the therapist's acceptance and empathy, through which Rogers believed that positive change was possible. Since therapy is client-centered, measures of success are taken from clients' descriptions of their "real" versus their "ideal" self at various points during therapy.

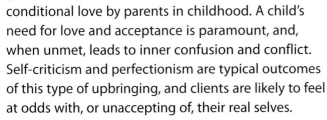

Empathy
The ability to understand and to share someone else's feelings.

The key relationship
The effectiveness of different types of therapy depends primarily on the client and the therapist forming a good working relationship. Empathy, genuineness, reassurance and support, and reinforcement by the therapist of the client's newly learned adaptive responses tend to be more important in producing change than the specific therapeutic method.

Physical Therapies

Psychotherapeutical approaches are not the only treatments available for mental disorders. The majority of people will be treated by a "physical" therapy or medication by their family doctor or a psychiatrist, or perhaps in the hospital.

The treatment of mental-health problems as a medical illness and the provision of hospital care and drugs are largely a product of Western history. During the 17th and 18th centuries, mental institutions used forms of physical treatment, such as harnesses and restraints, to pacify the most disturbed patients. Other inhumane treatments, such as revolving chairs and blindfolds, were used to "shock" people out of their madness. Some institutions used psychologically based treatments, such as mesmerism and hypnosis. However, many institutions were purely custodial and did not seek to treat or cure their inmates.

Birth of psychiatry

By the beginning of the 19th century, some doctors were questioning the inhumane treatment of inmates of mental institutions. This was the beginning of the medical discipline of psychiatry: Psychiatrists believed that mental disorders originated from a disease of the brain and the nervous system.

As drugs were developed during the 1950s, scientists hoped that many of the most serious mental disorders could be cured or their symptoms suppressed by medication. Similarly, as scientists discover more about the brain and neurotransmitters, they hope that certain mental disorders may be eliminated in the near future.

The medical model

The application of the medical model to mental-health problems was the most influential approach in the treatment of mental disorders in the 20th century.

Hypnosis

The induction of a state of mind in which someone loses the power of voluntary action and is highly responsive to suggestion.

Curriculum Context

Students may find it interesting to find out about the drugs that were developed to treat mental disorders in the earlier 20th century.

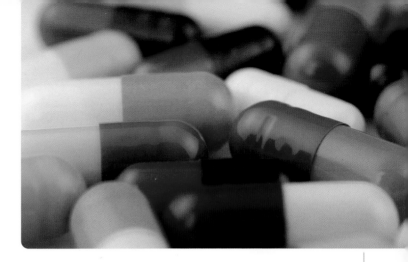

A large variety of drugs is available to treat many mental disorders. Doctors often prescribe medication since psychological services might not be readily available or entirely suitable for certain disorders.

The medical model assumes that mental disorders are caused by some malfunctioning or pathology of the brain, and that this shows up in two ways: signs and symptoms. Signs are objective indicators that the body is malfunctioning. Symptoms are feelings and sensations experienced by the patient.

The reliability problem

For mental disorders, however, there are very few objective tests that could detect reliable signs of an illness. The diagnosis is a judgment based on the doctor's knowledge and experience as to the underlying pathology or disease that might be affecting the patient.

Psychologists are frequently critical of the medical model and psychiatric diagnoses. Even if a diagnosis was reliable, it might not be very helpful in either deciding on the treatment or knowing the patient's prognosis. Many different mental disorders are treated with similar drugs or other forms of treatment.

Many psychologists stress that mental disorders can have several causes. Very few mental disorders have a specific biological cause or pathology that can be identified within an individual patient. Doctors and psychiatrists now generally accept that explanations of mental disorders need to include physical,

Pathology
Physical or mental disease.

Objective
Not influenced by personal feelings or opinions.

Curriculum Context

Students are expected to be able to explain the differences between psychology and psychiatry.

Psychiatry and Human Rights: A Brief History

19th century: Unmarried mothers and women who had many sexual partners were often detained in institutions for the insane or the mentally retarded.

1920s: The eugenics movement in the United States advocated the compulsory sterilization of people with certain mental disorders.

1930s and 1940s: In Nazi Germany people with serious mental disorders or retardation were put to death within medical institutions.

1950s: Homosexuality was considered a mental disorder and included as a psychiatric diagnosis.

1950s–1980s: In many communist regimes prior to the 1990s, political dissidents were detained in mental hospitals and treated against their will.

1990s: In the United Kingdom it was found that many young men from poor and ethnic minority backgrounds were frequently and forcibly treated for psychosis. It raised the issue of prejudice within mental-health services.

Curriculum Context

Students should appreciate why the most effective treatment of mental disorders will include good social care.

psychological, and cultural factors. Similarly, an effective treatment for a severe mental disorder will also include a combination of physical treatments, psychological interventions, and good social care.

This chapter looks at the more common medical, or physical, treatments used to relieve the suffering and symptoms of mental disorders.

Anxiety

Drugs that doctors commonly prescribe to treat anxiety are known as anxiolytics. The drugs are also often called tranquilizers. Anxiolytics are widely used to treat most types of anxiety, including anxiety that is associated with depression. The most commonly used anxiolytics are called benzodiazepines, such as diazepam (Valium) and lorazepam (Ativan).

Although such drugs are effective in damping down the symptoms of anxiety, when people try to stop taking them after longterm use, some develop withdrawal symptoms worse than the original anxiety. Withdrawal symptoms include panicky feelings, sleep problems, irritability, shakiness, and agitation. Most symptoms gradually wear off over a period of weeks or months, although in rare cases they can be more severe and include confusion or even epileptic fits. Some doctors feel that the problem has been exaggerated because the majority of patients do not get addicted to benzodiazepines. As a rule, however, doctors are now careful to prescribe benzodiazepines for a shorter time and in lower doses.

Antidepressants

When doctors think it essential to use drug treatment for anxiety, they usually recommend an antidepressant. Antidepressants were originally used for treating depression, but there is now a great deal of evidence that antidepressants, particularly the selective serotonin reuptake inhibitor, or SSRI, types, effectively treat generalized anxiety disorder, social phobia, agoraphobia, and panic disorder. The advantage of antidepressants is that they are not addictive. The disadvantage is that they have side effects.

Many mental-health professionals feel that people may become dependent on drugs to treat their symptoms when it would be better to learn new psychological ways of coping. Anxiety symptoms often stay with a person for years, and long-term drug treatment should be avoided whenever possible. Where drugs are thought necessary, they should be combined with psychological treatment.

Depression

Like anxiety, depression is regarded as clinical only when it becomes particularly severe and has some specific characteristics. Major depression is characterized by a persistent depressed mood and a loss of interest or pleasure in anything, together with other signs and symptoms, such as weight loss, sleep disturbance, lack of energy, feelings of guilt, and thoughts of suicide.

Epileptic
Relating to epilepsy, a disorder marked by convulsions or periods of loss of consciousness.

Curriculum Context

It is useful to know how benzodiazepines and SSRIs alter the chemistry of the brain in people with anxiety.

Vesicle

A small, fluid-filled sac within the body.

Mood and neurotransmitters

Neurotransmitters are contained in vesicles in nerve endings. When a nerve impulse travels along a nerve cell, the transmitter is released into the synaptic gap, the space between two nerve cells. The transmitter activates specific receptors on the next nerve cell, generating another nerve impulse. Excess transmitter is actively taken back by the first nerve cell.

Certain neurotransmitters, particularly noradrenaline and serotonin, play an important part in controlling mood. After the discovery by chance in the 1950s of the first antidepressants—tricyclics and MAOIs— scientists recognized that the drugs were acting through their effect on these neurotransmitters. A lot of research went into finding new drugs that would act on only one neurotransmitter.

A nerve impulse traveling along a nerve cell releases the neurotransmitter into the synaptic gap between two nerve cells. Normally, appropriate receptors on another nerve would absorb some of the neurotransmitter, and the rest would be taken back into the original nerve. An SSRI blocks this reabsorbtion, so the neurotransmitter stays longer in the gap and has greater effect on mood.

Selective neurotransmitter reuptake

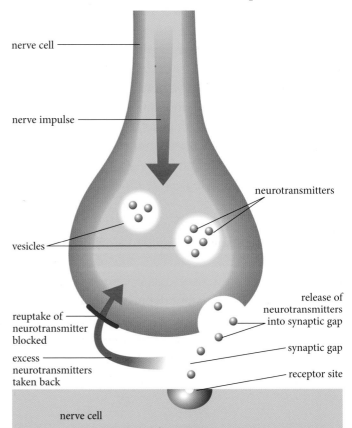

nerve cell

nerve impulse

neurotransmitters

vesicles

reuptake of neurotransmitter blocked

excess neurotransmitters taken back

release of neurotransmitters into synaptic gap

synaptic gap

receptor site

nerve cell

The research led to a whole new group of drugs called the selective serotonin reuptake inhibitors (SSRI). Tricyclic and SSRI antidepressants act by blocking the reuptake of neurotransmitters so that more remains in the synapse (the junction of two nerve cells) for a longer period of time and has a prolonged effect. Tricyclic antidepressants block both noradrenaline and serotonin reuptake, but SSRI drugs govern the reuptake of serotonin more than that of noradrenaline. MAOIs work by blocking the enzyme monoamine oxidase, which breaks down the neurotransmitters inside the cells.

Enzyme
A substance produced by a living organism that brings about a biochemical reaction.

Prozac

The most widely used of the SSRIs is fluoxetine, best known as Prozac. Because SSRI drugs have fewer harmful effects on the heart and other body organs, these drugs are safer in overdose than the older tricyclic antidepressants. Despite this, the SSRI drugs do have some disadvantages. A small number of people develop nausea or even vomiting while taking these drugs. There are also reports of increased aggression and suicidal impulses in a few people taking Prozac. Tricyclic antidepressants have other side effects, including a dry mouth, weight gain, and effects on blood pressure and heart rate. MAOIs are not much used now because they have dangerous side effects.

Treatment with SSRIs

It takes two or three weeks for an antidepressant to have full effect. Even then, only about two-thirds of patients will see significant benefit. In some cases, treatment for as long as four or six weeks might be necessary to get any benefit. If the first antidepressant does not work after that length of time, then the doctor will normally try a different antidepressant. Once the patient responds to it, treatment is normally continued for around six months after a single episode of acute depression. Without this prolonged treatment,

Curriculum Context

It may be interesting for students to look up data on the safety or otherwise of SSRIs.

depression will return in around 50 percent of patients; that rate falls to 15 percent in patients who are given continuation treatment. People who develop chronic or recurring depression might need antidepressant treatment for much longer.

It is seldom enough to use antidepressants as the only way of treating depression. Many people with milder forms of the disorder will do well with simple explanation, support, and reassurance without the need for medication at all. Even more serious forms of depression can often be treated using a form of psychotherapy known as cognitive therapy. Also, many bouts of depression are caused by an adverse life event. After time, many people might get over such adverse events either by coming to terms with their loss, or some other event might happen in their life that compensates for the original negative event. It is, therefore, necessary to discuss this with the patient. Most often a combination of antidepressant treatment with psychological therapy is the preferred way of treating moderate to severe degrees of depression.

Prozac Nation

It is suggested that many people receiving SSRIs are doing so to lift their mood rather than to diminish their depression, and that people who are not clinically depressed are prescribed SSRIs to enhance their mood. Is this any different from some people taking illegal substances to "get their kicks"? It raises the possibility of lifestyle or mood-altering drugs that could be legally prescribed in addition to those traditionally used, such as caffeine, alcohol, and nicotine.

Antipsychotic drugs

Antipsychotic drugs, or neuroleptics, are used to treat psychotic disorders such as schizophrenia. Schizophrenia is a diagnostic term that probably covers a range of disorders that psychiatrists also describe as psychosis. The disorders are characterized by major disturbances of thinking and perception—including hallucinations and delusions—together with emotional disturbances that make social contact difficult. It is commonly held that several different types of schizophrenia exist, so it is likely that no single treatment approach will be successful.

Antipsychotic drugs were discovered in the 1950s. They are now known as typical antipsychotics. They are thought to work by blocking dopamine D2 receptors in the brain. Scientists used to think that schizophrenia was caused by overactivity of dopamine systems in the brain. They came to believe this because antipsychotic drugs block dopamine receptors; and drugs, such as amphetamines, that stimulate dopamine activity can cause symptoms similar to those experienced in schizophrenia. Also, when scientists studied brain tissue taken from schizophrenic patients after death, they found that there were an excessive number of dopamine receptors. However, it now seems that this increased number of dopamine receptors was mainly caused by the drugs. If you block dopamine receptors, then your body responds by making more. Modern studies using brain-imaging techniques in living patients suggest that changes in brain dopamine function are very small in people with schizophrenia who are not taking drugs.

Newer antipsychotic drugs, which are known as atypical, have less effect on dopamine receptors and also act on other receptors, including those for serotonin. Many doctors claim that atypical antipsychotics are more effective treatments and cause fewer side effects.

Using antipsychotics

Antipsychotic drugs are used in three ways. First, large doses of antipsychotic drugs are sometimes given to control very disturbed behavior. This type of use of the drugs has been called a chemical baton or chemical straitjacket by those who oppose the use of drugs to treat psychiatric disorders.

The next phase of treatment lasts for a month or so, when antipsychotic drugs are given on a regular basis to reduce the severity of positive symptoms such as delusions and hallucinations. It is usually the positive symptoms that mostly respond at this stage of treatment. The negative symptoms, such as lack of drive and motivation and reduced emotional responses, slowly become more disabling and might prevent the person from making a full recovery. Unfortunately, negative symptoms are less easily treated by medication.

Compliance is a major factor in the effectiveness of drug treatment. If patients do not take their medication as prescribed—perhaps because they do not understand how it works—they will not fully benefit from it.

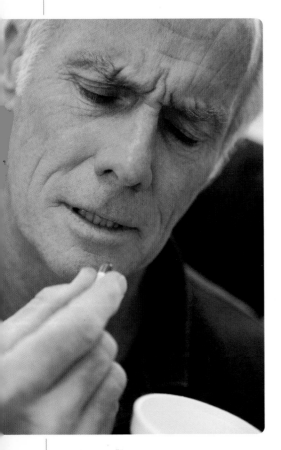

The third stage is long-term treatment with medication that is aimed at reducing the risk of relapse. This does not fit with our usual view of medication and why we take pills, however. When their psychotic symptoms get better, most people want to stop taking the medication. That is usually because they want to reduce the side effects and because most people are very reluctant to take medication throughout their lives. Stopping medication usually results in a relapse in the disorder at some time over the following few months.

Side effects of antipsychotics

The main side effects of the older, typical antipsychotic drugs are muscle stiffness and shaking similar to Parkinson's disease. Long-term treatment can cause a disorder known as tardive dyskinesia, which mostly affects the mouth and face with involuntary movements such as grimacing or twitching. The newer, atypical antipsychotic drugs have side effects of their own, such as weight gain.

Clozapine has been shown to be the most effective antipsychotic drug. However, it carries the risk of reducing the white cell count in the blood to a level at which patients can get infections that, in rare cases, can be fatal. Because of this, doctors treating patients with clozapine monitor them very carefully with regular blood tests and only use the drug if other antipsychotics have not worked.

Limitations of antipsychotics

Antipsychotic drugs are not curative. They mainly suppress symptoms and delay relapse. About a third of patients do not respond adequately to them. Even with the most effective use of drug treatment, many people with schizophrenia have long-term disability caused by continuing symptoms, particularly the so-called negative symptoms. In fact, the long-term outcome of schizophrenia in terms of this residual (remaining) disability has not changed substantially since antipsychotic drugs were introduced. Many patients will eventually show a relapse of the acute psychotic symptoms that might lead to further hospital admissions. The advantage of using the drugs, however, is that they allow patients to be treated without being hospitalized, because the drugs damp down the more obvious symptoms that lead to disturbed behavior.

Mood-stabilizing drugs

Doctors prescribe mood-stabilizing drugs to help patients who show mood swings either upward (mania) or downward (depression) on a regular basis. Typically, these types of mood swing last for weeks or months, with periods of normality in between.

Dyskinesia
Abnormality or impairment of voluntary movement.

Curriculum Context

Since antipsychotic drugs are not curative, students should consider other therapies that might be more effective in the treatment of mental disorders, such as schizophrenia.

Curriculum Context

Students should be able to explain the biological reasons why lithium helps in the treatment of bipolar 1 disorder.

In the past the most commonly used drug for treating the mood swings of bipolar 1 disorder was lithium. There is good evidence that long-term treatment with lithium will reduce the frequency of mood swings. Lithium, however, does have side effects: If its level in the blood gets too high, then symptoms such as shakiness and diarrhea become more common. Very high lithium levels can cause toxicity leading to convulsions and even death. Lithium levels in the

Licensing Drugs

For many years clinical scientists have conducted drug trials to assess the effectiveness of individual drugs and also to measure their side effects. A new drug is usually tested against an existing treatment or against a control or placebo treatment that is not expected to yield any positive effects. Usually these trials are conducted "double blind," so that neither the patient nor the clinician knows what type of medication the patient is receiving.

The results of these randomized control trials now greatly influence the choice of particular treatments for individual disorders. Politicians argue that money should only be invested in treatments that have been scientifically proven to be effective. In the United States it is part of the managed care movement: Doctors need to account for their choice of treatments to an insurance company, which usually picks up the bill for the patient's treatment.

blood have to be measured on a regular basis. Lithium is still widely used, but other treatments are now finding favor. Doctors prefer anticonvulsant drugs, which are normally used for epilepsy.

Electroconvulsive therapy (ECT)
In 1935, Ladislaus Meduna found that patients with psychotic symptoms who also suffered from epilepsy showed reduced psychotic symptoms after an epileptic fit. He therefore induced convulsions in the patients by giving them a brain convulsant, cardiazol, to mimic epilepsy in the belief that one disorder would chase out the other.

In 1938 Ugo Cerletti and Lucio Bini brought about convulsions in patients by applying an electric current across the temples. This treatment is now known as electroconvulsive therapy (ECT). Patients are given an anesthetic injection into a vein so they are not conscious during the procedure, and then given a further injection to relax the muscles. Because of this the body does not convulse, even though the brain shows signs of epileptic activity after the electric shock has been administered. Often six or eight electric shocks are given in total, spaced out at a rate of two or three times per week.

There is evidence that ECT can be effective for severe depression during which patients' lives might be threatened, not only from suicide but also if they lapse into a stupor and cannot eat or drink. ECT is potentially lifesaving in such situations. Some psychiatrists will also use ECT for less severe forms of depression when other treatments have not been effective. One problem with using ECT in this way is that it generally brings only short-term benefit. It is still necessary to use medication on a longer-term basis in order the prevent the depression from returning.

Stupor

A state of near unconsciousness or insensibility.

Studies comparing sham ECT (in which the anaesthetic is given without the electroshock) have shown that much of the benefit occurs with the sham treatment. After three months there is no difference in the outcome between the real and the sham procedures.

Curriculum Context

Many curricula expect students to appreciate the history of ECT use and why it is so controversial.

There is also controversy about the potential long-term harmful effects of ECT. Sometimes treatment can be followed by a short period of poor memory and mental confusion. Some patients claim that their memory and other intellectual functions have been permanently impaired. For many patients it is still a deeply distressing form of treatment.

Mental Disorders and Society

Since the beginning of the 20th century society has viewed mental disorder in many different ways. The story of mental disorders in modern society is a vivid tale of therapists and scientists wrestling with complex problems that have no easy solutions.

For the greater part of the 20th century, psychoanalytic theory about mental disorders was most influenced by the work of Sigmund Freud (1856–1939). According to Freud, all psychological disorders are rooted in unconscious conflicts—internal mental battles that occur outside of awareness and eventually lead to depression, phobias, eating disorders, and even severe mental disorders, such as schizophrenia. From the perspective of mental disorders and society, one aspect of his theory stands out: Freud was the first researcher to develop a model of mental disorders that was almost entirely psychological.

Rise of drug treatments

The first psychotropic drugs became available even before Freud was constructing his revolutionary model of the mind. But it was not until the early 1950s, with the release of a medication called haloperidol, that drug treatments assumed a major role in the treatment of mental disorders. Haloperidol was the first widely prescribed antipsychotic medication. By removing the hallucinations (false perceptions) and delusions (false beliefs) caused by schizophrenia, haloperidol has given many severely disturbed patients their first real opportunity to live on their own outside the confines of a hospital ward.

The widespread use of antipsychotic medications resulted in a 90 percent reduction in the mental hospital population. But where did all these patients go—and were they cured? Ex-patients found follow-up services hard to come by, and without guidance and

Psychotropic drugs
Medications used to treat mental disorders.

supervision many with serious mental disorders simply stopped taking their medication. They drifted onto the fringes of society, too confused (and sometimes too ashamed) to seek medical and psychiatric help on their own. Many of the patients released from mental hospitals during the 1950s through to the 1970s ended up on the streets. The problem has worsened over the years. Research shows that 30 percent or more of homeless people suffer from at least one serious mental disorder. The decline of mental hospitals and the resulting increase in homelessness illustrate one of the fundamental truths about mental disorders: there are no ideal social solutions.

A relatively high proportion of homeless people suffer from mental disorders. Since the introduction of antipsychotic drugs in the 1950s, they are rarely taken into residential care.

Current perspectives

Under the influence of Freud, the first decades of the 20th century saw the rise of mind theories of mental disorders. The latter part of the century saw the increased use of drug treatments and biologically based brain theories. At first the two approaches were seen as alternatives, but increasingly they are regarded as complementary parts of a single whole.

Psychiatrists are physicians with special expertise in the biological aspects of mental disorders. Like other

Curriculum Context

Many curricula expect students to know the main psychological theories of mental disorders.

Psychiatrists are physicians who specialize in the physiological aspects of mental disorders. They are qualified to treat the symptoms with drugs, if necessary. Most psychiatrists work in hospitals, but many also see patients in private practice.

Curriculum Context

Students should be aware of the training required to become a psychiatrist.

doctors, they complete four years of medical school, but then move on to specialize in diagnosis and treatment of mental disorders. Until the 1970s psychiatrists provided both psychotherapy and medication, with different psychiatrists emphasizing different types of treatment depending on their own training and theoretical orientation. In fact, it was not unusual for psychiatrists to devote most of their efforts to psychotherapy, with very little time spent prescribing medication. Many used some version of Freud's theory in their therapeutic work. Since then the picture has changed dramatically. Psychiatrists now devote most of their time to prescribing and managing medications. Meanwhile, psychotherapy is provided by psychologists and psychotherapists.

General practitioners (family physicians) also play a greater role in the process than ever before, treating mental disorders with medication. They now receive extensive training in pharmacology. Because of this they are better able to treat mental disorders without the help of a psychiatrist. The latest medication has fewer side effects than earlier products and is therefore

Pharmacology

The scientific study of drugs and their effects.

easier to manage. Patients are more willing to take their medicine, and fewer discontinue their drugs against doctors' orders. Financial pressures from managed care organizations, such as insurance companies, have forced family physicians to handle by themselves some milder forms of mental disorders, such as moderate depression or anxiety.

Psychologists

For all the help that physicians now provide, most nonextreme mental disorders are handled by psychologists. Unlike psychiatrists, they rely on therapy alone. There are various approved methods and guidelines, the most important of which are contained in the *Diagnostic and Statistical Manual of Mental Disorders*. Through a combination of tests and careful listening, psychologists are able to make judgments about their patients' mental state and then, if necessary, refer them to a psychiatrist.

Psychologists typically undergo four years' graduate training, plus a one- or two-year internship in a hospital or similar establishment. They also receive extensive training in conducting and evaluating scientific research to keep abreast of the latest findings in their field. Some clinical psychologists continue to conduct research in hospitals and other treatment settings.

Different clinical psychologists have different theoretical orientations—they apply different models of the mind to psychotherapy. Three theoretical orientations are most popular among clinical psychologists—they are the psychodynamic, the behavioral, and the cognitive.

The psychodynamic orientation is essentially a modern version of Freud's psychoanalysis that emphasizes talking about patients' problems and helping them gain insight into the source of their current difficulties. The behavioral orientation focuses on helping the

Curriculum Context

Many curricula ask students to explain the therapies used in main branches of clinical psychology.

patient learn how to replace self-defeating behaviors with more adaptive behaviors. The cognitive orientation emphasizes changing patients' thought patterns to be more optimistic and realistic. Many clinical psychologists use bits and pieces of different theories in treating different patients, modifying their approach to suit each patient's needs.

The role of therapists

Since World War II, numerous other types of psychotherapist have appeared on the scene. In general these therapists have less extensive training than clinical psychologists or psychiatrists and handle a narrower range of patient problems. Some specialize in marriage guidance counseling and family therapy; others treat only people with addictive disorders, such as alcohol or drug addiction.

Curriculum Context

Students may find it useful to consider the importance of clinical social workers in the lives of people with mental disorders.

Clinical social workers often deal with cases of mental disorders in which factors such as financial and housing difficulties play a prominent role. In addition to doing traditional psychotherapy, social workers may help their patients gain access to social services such as housing assistance that they might not otherwise get.

The role of self-help programs

The first self-help program for a mental disorder, alcohol addiction, was Alcoholics Anonymous (AA), founded in 1935. AA is now so well established that virtually every city and most smaller communities have at least one active AA chapter. Like all self-help programs, AA emphasizes the need for individuals to take responsibility for their own recovery and support other people who are going through a similar struggle. Studies confirm that self-help programs of this type can be very effective in helping people recover from addiction. Other drug-related self-help programs based on AA principles have taken root, such as Cocaine Users Anonymous and Marijuana Users Anonymous.

Are We Getting Sicker?

Research shows that your parents are more likely to develop serious depression than your grandparents were, and that you are more likely to become depressed than your parents. If current trends continue, your children will be at higher risk of depression than you are, and your grandchildren's risk will be even higher. No one knows why this should be the case, but the fact remains that the incidence of depression is increasing with each passing generation.

Some researchers take the view that increased rates of mental disorders reflect our increased contact with environmental toxins—everything from air and water pollution to chemicals in the home. This increased exposure to potentially harmful chemicals begins even before we are born.

Other experts contend that these data are misleading. Mental disorders are not getting more common; we are just getting better at identifying them. People are more willing to talk about psychological problems than they used to be, and mental-health professionals are better at diagnosing them.

The self-help movement has branched out beyond addiction. There are groups for people who suffer from depression, anxiety, and eating disorders. They are also available for parents who are grieving the loss of a child and for children who are grieving the loss of a parent. Victims of physical and sexual abuse, people who care for relatives with Alzheimer's disease, children and adults with learning difficulties—all now have specialized self-help support groups available.

Curriculum Context

Students should consider the reasons people may benefit from membership of a self-help group.

The role of the community

People living in extreme poverty have little chance of receiving even basic medical care, let alone cutting-edge mental-health treatment. For such people, community outreach programs are critical. These initiatives—which are staffed by teams of mental-health professionals and located near the communities that need them most—do not wait for people to come and ask for help. Instead, they make the first contact themselves, through flyers, radio advertisements, even by going door-to-door. They want to make sure that everyone who needs their services knows how to get them.

Stressful social conditions such as poverty and poor housing have been shown to be major contributors to mental disorders. The community psychology—or primary prevention—movement aims to improve social conditions to reduce the risk of mental disorders within a community.

Curriculum Context

Students might be asked to examine the ways in which the primary prevention movement makes life less stressful for communities.

The primary prevention movement

Mental-health professionals have long known that stressful events, such as living in poverty, place people at increased risk of mental disorder. In the early 1960s George Albee (1921–2006) proposed that, instead of waiting for disorders to strike and then treating them, mental healthcare professionals should employ preventive measures so that there would be fewer disorders in the first place.

The primary prevention movement—sometimes called the community psychology movement—was born. Now psychologists and other mental-health professionals work with entire communities, trying to find ways of making life for the people less stressful and more pleasant. Studies show that Albee's primary prevention strategy works: When community stress is reduced, fewer people develop mental-health problems, and fewer need treatment.

The multipronged approach

The more we learn about different methods of treating mental illness, the easier it is to see that a given disorder might be treated in more than one way. Often a patient benefits most when several different forms of treatment are used in combination.

Today most disorders are treated using a multipronged strategy that addresses the biological, psychological, and environmental aspects of the disorder at the same time. Thus, for example, severely depressed people might receive antidepressant medication to deal with the biology of the disorder as well as traditional psychotherapy to address its psychological components. At the same time, psychologists and social workers will intervene wherever possible to change the patients' environment—to improve their living conditions and help them obtain better access to medical care and other social services.

Curriculum Context

Students may be expected to be aware of all the different options available to help people with mental disorders.

The role of technology

Technology has not only helped psychiatrists delve deeper, it has also enabled psychologists to reach out and connect with people who might not otherwise be able to obtain access to mental-health services. It is now possible for patients to receive psychotherapy over the Internet, conversing with psychologists who may be thousands of miles away. Housebound people and people living in isolated, rural areas have benefited tremendously from Internet-based therapy.

Confidentiality

Virtually everything that a patient says to a mental-health professional must be kept in strict confidence. It may not be revealed to anyone without the patient's permission—even to other treatment professionals or the patient's family. There are two exceptions to this rule, however. The first is when the patient reports that child abuse has occurred. In this case it does not matter whether the patient was the victim or the abuser; nor does it matter whether the abuse is continuing to happen or took place in the past. Neither does it matter whether the abuse was sexual, physical, or emotional. Once the patient discloses child abuse, the therapist has to report it right away to the child-abuse authorities.

Implausible

Not probable or failing to convince.

The other time that confidentiality must be broken is when a patient threatens to harm another person. The rules are strict: The patient must make a realistic threat against an identifiable person. Implausible threats made against unnamed people do not count.

Informed consent

Patients have the right to be informed about the risks and benefits of any treatment. They must be given accurate, unbiased information, and they have a right to ask questions until they are satisfied. The patient also has the right to be informed of other possible treatments, even if the psychologist or psychiatrist does not favor such treatments.

Patients must specifically consent to receive treatment after being informed of its potential benefits and risks, and they must give consent in writing before the treatment can begin. If patients choose not to receive a recommended treatment, that, too, is their right. Even after treatment has begun, they may change their minds and decide to stop it. The right holds regardless of whether patients are being treated in a doctor's office, in a clinic, or in a hospital.

Curriculum Context

Students should be able to identify conflicts between individual rights and the rights of society concerning mental health issues.

What happens when people's thoughts are so confused by schizophrenia or Alzheimer's disease, for example, that they cannot realistically give informed consent? In such cases another person (usually a family member) is appointed to do it for them. If a patient should later regain the ability to give informed consent, then the other person steps aside and the patient has the right to give or refuse consent.

Humane treatment

Patients with mental disorders also have the right to be dealt with humanely. They must be treated in the least restrictive environment possible. They may not be kept in locked wards unless keeping them in open wards would be dangerous. They may not be physically restrained unless they would otherwise do harm to themselves or other people. Under no circumstances may a patient be threatened, hit, or handled roughly.

The right to humane treatment extends to other areas as well. Patients must be allowed to receive visitors, to have social contact with other patients, to make and receive phone calls, and to attend religious services. Patients have a right to wear their own clothes and to decorate their rooms.

Cultural sensitivity

Statistical studies have shown that for many years members of ethnic minority groups in the United States, such as Asian and African Americans, were traditionally unwilling to seek treatment for mental disorders. This reluctance stemmed either from fear or from a cultural belief that such problems should be handled without professional help. Today, however, many more members of ethnic and racial minority

Curriculum Context

Some curricula ask students to explain why the cultural beliefs of certain ethnic groups may prevent them from seeking treatment for mental disorders.

Culture and Psychological Symptoms

Some psychological disorders, such as depression, turn up in almost every society. Other mental illnesses are found in some cultures but not in others. For example, bipolar 1 disorder was almost unheard of in Japan until the mid-20th century. Eating disorders such as anorexia and bulimia are extremely rare in many African nations. There is no doubt that culture affects mental disorders. In fact, some mental disorders are surprisingly culture specific. They turn up in one—and only one—society, and they seem to reflect something important about that society's traditions and values.

Here are two examples of mental disorders that are highly culture bound:
- *Dhat* syndrome in India is characterized by weakness, dizziness, insomnia, and bodily aches. It is thought to be caused by excessive loss of semen in men.
- *Taijin kyofusho* is a Japanese syndrome characterized by an intense fear that one's physical appearance, facial expression, and body odor are offensive to other people. It appears to stem from a deep-seated belief that one is not living in sufficient harmony with other members of the community.

groups seek treatment for mental disorders to get the help they need. As psychologists and psychiatrists deal with an increasingly diverse patient population, they have had to become more sensitive to cultural values and cultural norms. Behavior that will pass without remark in one culture may be regarded as disturbed if done in another. It is important that mental-health professionals bear this in mind and do not try to force their own beliefs onto patients. Instead, they must respect the patients' right to handle their own problems however they choose.

Legal issues

People with mental illnesses have the right to make informed decisions about themselves and their care. But there are exceptions to this rule. The main one occurs when patients are so seriously impaired by the symptoms of their disorder that they cannot make reasonable, informed decisions on their own behalf. When this occurs, they may be declared legally incompetent, and others will be designated to make decisions for them. Such a person—known as a guardian—is appointed by the courts through a formal legal process known as a "competency hearing." The guardian is expected to make decisions that are in the other person's best interests.

Having a person declared legally incompetent is not a simple matter. Evidence of legal incompetence must be compelling, and courts are usually reluctant to declare someone legally incompetent unless failure to do so would clearly put the person at risk. Competency hearings can be lengthy, expensive, and complicated, with psychologists and psychiatrists presenting evidence on both sides.

Simply because people are declared incompetent today does not mean they will still be incompetent next week or next month. Follow-up court hearings

Curriculum Context

Students should be able to explain the difficulties experts face in deciding whether a patient is legally competent.

must be held periodically to give them the chance to demonstrate that they have regained their competence and can again make informed decisions on their own.

People cannot be declared incompetent simply because their beliefs are strange or unusual. Similarly, if people refuse lifesaving medical treatment on religious grounds, they are entitled to do so.

Involuntary commitment

Involuntary commitment occurs when people are hospitalized against their will. People may be involuntarily committed only under certain very specific circumstances. They must be a clear and immediate danger either to themselves or to other people or they must be unable to care for themselves.

Once people have been involuntarily committed to a psychiatric hospital, steps must be taken to ensure that they are treated fairly and humanely. For example, civil commitment lasts only for a short time—48 or 72 hours in most states—and at the end of the period patients have the right to be released from the hospital unless staff can prove that they are still a danger to

In 1960 Thomas Szasz (born 1920) published a paper, "The Myth of Mental Illness," in which he argued that mental illness does not really exist—it is an idea made up to explain behavior that seems irrational ("crazy") to most members of society. We all have a right to be as strange as we please, he argues, as long as we do not interfere with anyone else. Mental-health professionals have no right to force people to give up their strange behaviors no matter how self-destructive those behaviors might be.

themselves or others. People who are involuntarily hospitalized have exactly the same rights as people who go in voluntarily. They have the right to therapist–patient confidentiality, to make informed decisions regarding their care, to refuse treatment they do not want, and to be treated with respect and dignity.

The future

How will mental disorders be viewed and treated in our society in the future? It was not that long ago that people with mental disorders were routinely discriminated against in the workplace. As recently as the 1970s, people in the public eye tried to hide the fact that they were receiving mental-health treatment for fear their careers would be jeopardized. Since then things have changed. People with mental disorders are much more willing to talk about their experiences,

Curriculum Context

Many curricula ask students to discuss the stigma associated with abnormal behavior.

A Right to Be Crazy?

In the late 1980s Joyce Brown lived on the Upper East Side of Manhattan in one of New York City's most exclusive and expensive neighborhoods. The problem was, Joyce Brown lived on the street. She refused to live quietly in the shadows, as many homeless people do. Instead, she made a scene. She talked to herself, paced the streets gesturing wildly, and urinated and defecated in public. She begged for money; but if anyone gave her a dollar or two, she burned the cash. Residents began to complain about Brown's behavior, and nearby businesses complained that she was driving away customers. Eventually the police arrested her, and she was committed to a psychiatric hospital. She was deemed legally incompetent and forced to receive treatment, including antipsychotic medication.

Joyce Brown found a sympathetic attorney who accepted her argument that she had a right to live her life however she wanted. Brown brought suit against the City of New York for violating her civil rights by forcing her off the street and onto medication—and she won. Although she was not permitted to behave antisocially (urinating in public is illegal), the courts found that otherwise she did indeed have the right to live however she wanted as long as she did not interfere with other people's right to live peacefully as well.

The case of Joyce Brown has important implications for the civil rights of people with serious mental disorders. It points out that simply because people have a mental disorder it does not mean they can be told where (and how) to live.

and by doing so, they make it easier for others to talk about theirs too.

Things have also changed in the legal arena. With the passing of the 1990 Americans with Disabilities Act (ADA), it became illegal to discriminate on the basis of any type of illness, physical or mental. Increasingly, mental disorders have come to be seen as challenges, not weaknesses or flaws. And just as employers must accommodate workers who have physical challenges, they must accommodate those who have mental challenges to overcome.

Improved diagnosis and treatment techniques— along with landmark laws such as the ADA—have brought mental disorders out of the closet and into mainstream society. As public perceptions change, mental disorders are no longer seen as barriers to success. In fact, the more we learn about mental disorders, the clearer it becomes that sometimes a successful struggle against a mental disorder can actually work in a person's favor. Many people with mental disorders have done outstanding creative work. And, as people who have overcome the challenge of mental disorders point out, once you have battled serious depression, life's everyday troubles do not seem so overwhelming.

We have made tremendous progress in dealing with mental disorders since the mid-20th century, but further challenges remain. The more we learn about mental disorders and accommodating them in society, the more we realize ideal solutions rarely exist. Society still has a responsibility, however, to find out as much as it can and to use the knowledge to deal more effectively with the disorders. Only by understanding the scientific and legal aspects of mental disorders can we make good decisions about the complex problems that will always confront us in this area.

Curriculum Context

Students should be aware of the very latest research into the effectiveness of current approaches in the treatment of mental disorders.

Glossary

Adaptive Able to adjust to new conditions.

Adolescence The period following the onset of puberty during which a child becomes an adult.

Adrenal Relating to a pair of ductless glands above the kidneys.

Agoraphobia The extreme or irrational fear of being alone and helpless in an inescapable situation; it is especially characterized by fear of open or public places.

Agoraphobics People suffering from agoraphobia.

AIDS A disease in which there is a severe loss of the body's cellular immunity.

Amphetamine An addictive, mood-altering drug, used as a stimulant.

Analysand A person undergoing psychoanalysis.

Antecedent Relating to something that existed before or logically proceeds another.

Aphasia Problems of comprehension and expression.

Atrophy The wasting away or shrinkage of brain tissue.

Atypical Not representative of a type.

Authoritarian Enforcing obedience to authority, at the expense of personal freedom.

Autonomic nervous system
The communication network by which the brain controls all parts of the body except for contraction of skeletal muscles.

Autopsies Examinations of dead bodies to discover the cause of death or the extent of disease.

Biochemical Concerned with the chemical processes that occur within living organisms.

Catatonic Immobile or unresponsive.

Chromosome A threadlike structure, consisting of DNA and proteins, found in the nucleus of cells.

Cognition The processing of information by the brain.

Concussion Temporary unconsciousness caused by a blow to the head.

Conformity Compliance with laws, rules, or standards.

Correlate To have a connection in which one thing affects or depends on another.

Cortex The outer layer of the brain that is concerned with consciousness.

Dissipate To break up and drive off.

Dyskinesia Abnormality or impairment of voluntary movement.

Ego The part of the psyche that distinguishes between the self and the real world.

Empathy The ability to understand and to share someone else's feelings.

Enzyme A substance produced by a living organism that brings about a biochemical reaction.

Epileptic Relating to epilepsy, a disorder marked by convulsions or periods of loss of consciousness.

Euphoria A state of intense excitement or happiness.

Exorcise To attempt to drive out an evil spirit.

Fast To abstain from food or drink, especially as a religious observance.

Gender The state of being either male or female.

Gene A unit of heredity that determines some specific characteristic and that is passed from parent to offspring.

Hallucinations Perceptions of objects, people, or events that have no basis in reality.

Heat stroke Excessive exposure to the sun and high temperatures.

HIV A virus that inserts its own genetic material into its hosts cells and which causes AIDS.

Hyperactivity Abnormal or extreme activity.

Hypnosis The induction of a state of mind in which someone loses the power of voluntary action and is highly responsive to suggestion.

Hypothesis Proposed explanation based on limited evidence and used as the starting point for further investigation.

Hysteria Physical ailments with no apparent cause, but thought to be related to the possession of a uterus and, therefore, exclusive to women.

Implausible Not probable or failing to convince.

IQ Intelligence quotient; a number representing someone's intelligence, as measured using problem-solving tests.

Irrational Not logical or reasonable.

Logical Concerning reasoning conducted according to strict rules of validity.

Maladaptive Not adjusting appropriately to a situation.

Manifestation A symptom or sign of an ailment.

Meningitis Inflammation of the meninges, which are membranes that line the skull and enclose the brain.

Metabolic Concerning the chemical processes within an organism that maintain life.

Motor skills The ability to control the muscles well.

Narcissism Extreme selfishness, with a grandiose view of one's own talents and a craving for admiration.

Neologisms Made-up, private words that others cannot understand without explanation.

Neurosis A mild mental illness involving symptoms of stress.

Neurotransmitters The chemicals that transfer impulses from one nerve fiber to another.

Objective Not influenced by personal feelings or opinions.

Paranoid Unreasonably or obsessively anxious, suspicious, or mistrustful.

Parotid glands A pair of large salivary glands just in front of each ear.

Pathology Physical or mental disease.

Peers People of the same age, status, or ability.

Peptides Compounds consisting of two or more amino acids.

Perseverate To repeat words or phrases again and again.

Pharmacology The scientific study of drugs and their effects.

Phobia An extreme or irrational fear of something.

Postmortem An examination of a dead body to establish the cause of death.

Psychodynamic Concerning the interrelation of the unconscious and conscious mental and emotional forces that determine personality and motivation.

Psychotropic drugs Medications used to treat mental disorders.

Sanctioned Given official permission or approval.

Schema A model or outline of a theory.

Sedatives Drugs taken for their calming or sleep-inducing effect.

Self-consciousness The knowledge of oneself as a conscious being.

Senile plaques Areas of nerve-cell loss and waxy deposits termed amyloids.

Sociological Concerning human society, its structure, and how it functions.

Stimulants Substances that raise levels of physiological or nervous activity in the body.

Stupor A state of near unconsciousness or insensibility.

Subjective Influenced by personal feelings or opinions.

Synapses Junctions between nerve cells in the brain.

Syndrome A condition characterized by a set of associated symptoms.

Thyroid A large, ductless gland in the neck.

Vesicle A small, fluid-filled sac within the body.

Further Research

BOOKS

American Psychiatric Association. *Diagnostic and Statistical Manual of Mental Disorders, 4th edition, Text Revision*. Washington, DC: American Psychiatric Press, 2000.

Brown, D. S. *Learning a Living: A Guide to Planning Your Career and Finding a Job for People with Learning Disabilities, Attention Deficit Disorder, and Dyslexia*. Bethesda, MD: Woodbine House, 2000.

Carson, R. C., Butcher, J. N., J. M. Hooley, and Mineka, S. *Abnormal Psychology, S.O.S. edition (12th edition)*. Upper Saddle River, NJ: Prentice Hall, 2004.

Cavan, S. *Recovery from Drug Addiction*. New York: Rosen Publishing Group, 2000.

Davis, R. D., and Braun, E. M. *The Gift of Dyslexia: Why Some of the Smartest People Can't Read and How They Can Learn*. New York: Perigee, 2010.

Kring, A., Johnson, S., Davison, G. C. , and Neal, J. M. *Abnormal Psychology (11th edition)*. New York: John Wiley and Sons, Inc., 2009.

Faherty, C. and Mesibov, G. B. *Asperger's: What Does It Mean to Me?* Arlington, TX: Future Horizons, 2000.

Fernando, S. and Keating, F. *Mental Health in a Multi-Ethnic Society: A Multi-Disciplinary Handbook (2nd edition)*. New York: Routledge, 2008.

Giacobello, J. *Everything You Need to Know about Anxiety and Panic Attacks*. New York: Rosen Publishing Group, 2000.

Grandin, T. *Thinking in Pictures: My Life with Autism*. New York: Vintage Books, 2010.

Hyde, M. O. and Setano, J. F. *When the Brain Dies First*. New York: Franklin Watts Inc., 2000.

Kaplan, H. I. and Sadock, B. J. *Synopsis of Psychiatry: Behavioral Sciences, Clinical Psychiatry*. Philadelphia, PA: Lippincott, Williams and Wilkins, 2007.

Mazziotta, J .C., Toga, A. W., and Frackowiak, R. S. J. (eds.). *Brain Mapping: The Disorders*. San Diego, CA: Academic Press, 2000.

Nadeau, K. G., Littman, E., and Quinn, P. O. *Understanding Girls with ADHD*. Niagara Falls, NY: Advantage Books, 2000.

Ogden, J. A. *Fractured Minds: A Case-study Approach to Clinical Neuropsychology*. New York: Oxford University Press, 2005.

Sarason, I. G. and Sarason, B. R. *Abnormal Psychology: The Problem of Maladaptive Behavior (11th edition)*. Upper Saddle River, NJ: Prentice Hall, 2004.

Segal, N. L. *Entwined Lives: Twins and What They Tell Us about Human Behavior*. New York: Plume, 2000.

Shorter, E. *Before Prozac: The Troubled History of Mood Disorders in Psychiatry*. New York: Oxford University Press, 2008.

Sommers, M. A. *Everything You Need to Know about Bipolar Disorder and Depressive Illness*. New York: Rosen Publishing Group, 2002.

Zarit, S. H. and Zarit, J. M. *Mental Disorders in Older Adults: Fundamentals of Assessment and Treatment. New York:* Guilford Press, 2006.

INTERNET RESOURCES

Alzheimer's Association. Information explaining Alzheimer's disease and how it affects the brain, and describing the treatments available.
www.alz.org

American Psychological Association. Here you can read follow the development of new ethical guidelines for psychologists, and find a wealth of other information.
www.apa.org

Association for Behavioral and Cognitive Therapies. An interdisciplinary organization concerned with the application of behavioral and cognitive sciences to the understanding of human behavior.
www.abct.org

Bedlam. The Museum of London's online exhibition about Bedlam, the notorious mental institution.
www.museum-london.org.uk/MOLsite/exhibits/bedlam/f_bed.htm

Freud and Culture. An online Library of Congress exhibition that examines Sigmund Freud's life and key ideas and his effect on 20th-century thinking.
www.loc.gov/exhibits/freud

Kidspsych. American Psychological Association's children's site, with games and exercises for kids.
www.kidspsych.org/index1.html

National Eating Disorders Society. Information on eating disorders, their precursors, how to help a friend, and the importance of treatment.
www.nationaleatingdisorders.org

Neuroscience for Kids. A useful website for students and teachers who want to learn about the nervous system. Enjoy activities and experiments on your way to learning all about the brain and spinal cord.
faculty.washington.edu/chudler/neurok.html

Neuroscience Tutorial. The Washington University School of Medicine's online tutorial offers an illustrated guide to the basics of clinical neuroscience, with useful artworks and user-friendly text.
thalamus.wustl.edu/course

Personality Theories. An electronic textbook covering personality theories for undergraduate and graduate courses.
www.ship.edu/~cgboeree/perscontents.html

Schizophrenia.com. Information and resources on this mental disorder provided by a charitable organization.
www.schizophrenia.com

Social Psychology Network. One of the largest social psychology databases on the Internet. Within these pages you will find more than 5,000 links to psychology-related resources and research groups, and there is also a useful section on general psychology.
www.socialpsychology.org

Index

Page numbers in *italic* refer to illustrations and captions.

A

abnormality 6–15
    definition of 6–7
acetylcholine 42, 44
acquired immune deficiency
        syndrome (AIDS) 43
addiction 36–39, *37*
adrenal dysfunction 27
adrenal glands 35
agoraphobia 18, 27, 83
Albee, George 98
alcohol 37, 38, 44, 45, 86
Alcoholics Anonymous (AA) 96
Alpha to Omega method 58, *58*
aluminum 42
Alzheimer, Alois 40
Alzheimer's disease (DAT) 13,
        40–42
    familial 40–41
    sporadic 40–41
American Psychiatric Association
        11
Americans with Disabilities Act
        (ADA) 1990 105
amphetamines 39
anger 30
anorexia nervosa 33–36
antidepressant medication 29
antisocial personality disorder
        10
anxiety 18
anxiety disorders 18–22, 75,
        82–83
aphasia 40
applied behavior analysis 51–53,
        52
arachnophobia *19*
asylums (mental institutions) 16,
        17, 80, 92–93
Ativan 82
attention deficit disorder 62
attention deficit hyperactivity
        disorder (ADHD) 60–64
attentional difficulties 22,
        60–62
autism 47–54, *49, 51,* 54, *55*
autonomic nervous system 20

B

Barchas, Jack D 65
basal ganglia 42
Bateson, Gregory 26
Beck, Aaron 21, 31
Bedlam 17

behavior
    adaptive 8, 69
    effect of culture on *8, 9,* 12,
        15
    effect of society groups on 8
    maladaptive 8–9, 11, 69
Bender, Bruce 56
benzodiazepines 82–83
Bini, Lucio 91
bipolar 1 disorder 32–33, *33,* 90,
        101
Bleuler, Eugene 22
brain 13, 20, 35, 40, 42, 43,
        50–51, 56–58, *57,* 62–63,
        64, 80, 81, 87
Briquet's syndrome 24
Brown, Joyce 104
bulimia nervosa 33–36, *35*

C

caffeine 86
cannabis 38–39
cardiazol 90
casein 51
caudate nucleus 63, *63*
cerebellum 51
Cerletti, Ugo 91
child abuse 99
Civil Rights movement 10
clinical social workers 96
clozapine 89
cocaine 39
cognitive behavioral therapy
        (CBT) 75–76, *75*
cognitive errors 29
cognitive triad 31
community outreach programs
        97
computed tomography (CT)
        scans 51
conditioning 69
confidentiality 99–100
conformity 10
corpus callosum 62–63
corpus striatum 63
cortex 42
criminal justice system 6

D

Decker, Sadie 56
deep white matter 42
delirium 43–45
delirium tremens 45
delusions 16, 22–23, 24, 40, 87,
        88, 92
    of control 22–23
    of grandeur 22

of persecution 22
of reference 22
dementias 13, 39–43
    subcortical 42–43
    vascular 42
depression 27–33, *31,* 39, 75, 77,
        83–86, 97
desensitization 70–71, *70, 75,*
        76
dhat syndrome 101
Diagnostic and Statistical Manual
        (DSM) 7, 11–12, 18, 47
diazepam (Valium) 82
distress 9–10
dopamine 25, 28–29, 63, 64,
        87
double-bind hypothesis 26
dreams 30, 66
drug trials 90
drugs 36–39
    medical *81, 88*
        amphetamines 64, 87
        anticonvulsant 90
        antidepressants 83–86
        antidepressants, MAOIs
            84, 85
        antidepressants, selective
            serotonin reuptake
            inhibitors (SSRIs) 83,
            84, 85–86
        antidepressants, tricyclics
            84, 85
        antipsychotic 86–89,
            92–93
        anxiolytics (tranquillizers)
            82–83
        licensing 90
        mood-stabilizing drugs
            89–90
        Prozac 29
        Ritalin 64
dyscalculia 54
dysgraphia 54–55
dyslexia 54–60, *57*

E

eating disorders 8, *8,* 33–36,
        101
echolalia 48
ectopias 57
ego 14, 25, 66, 67
ego analysts 68–69
electroconvulsive therapy (ECT)
        90–91
Ellis, Albert 74–75
endocrine system 35
Epidemiologic Catchment Area
        Study 7

P

panic attacks 21–22, 82
panic disorder 18, 83
paranoia 8, 39, 44
Parkinson's disease 42
Parks, Rosa 10
parotid glands 34
Peek, Kim 55
peer pressure 37
pharmacology 94
phobias 18–19, 19, *21, 70,* 71
   social 19, 83
   specific 18–19, *19,* 77
phonology 56
Pick's bodies 43
Pick's disease 43
pituitary gland 35
planum temporale 56–57, *57*
possession by evil spirits 14, 16
post–traumatic stress disorder
   (PTSD) *12,* 19–20, 77
primary narcissism 26
primary prevention movement
   (community psychology
   movement) 98, *98*
Prozac 29, 85
psychiatry 80, 82, 93–94, *94*
psychoanalysis 14, 66–69, 75, 92
psychologists 13, 46

R

Rain Man 55
rational emotive therapy (RET)
   74–75
reinforcement 52
religion 9, 14, 16, 103
Ritalin 64

Rogers, Carl 79
Roman philosophers and
   physicians 16
Rush, Benjamin 17
Rutter, Michael 50

S

savant syndrome 54
schizophrenia 22–26, *22,* 86–88,
   92
   catatonic 23–24
   hebephrenic 23
   paranoid 24
sedatives 39
self-constructs 72, 73
self-help programs 96–97
Seligman, Martin 32
sensitization 70, *70*
serotonin 28–29, 33, 63, 83, 84,
   85, 87
shaping 52–53
sleep problems *27,* 28, 39, 82
social acceptability 10
social norms 10, 26, 35
somatoform disorders 24
speech, disorganized 22, 23
stimulants 39
stimulus–response (S–R)
   psychology 69
studies
   adoption 25
   animal 32, 57
   family 20, 24–25, 29–30
   twin 20, 25, 29–30, 33, 37, 50,
      56, 63–64
substance abuse 36–39
suicide 83, 85
Sullivan, Joseph 55

superego 14, 66, 67
support groups 65
Szasz, Thomas *103*

T

taijin kyofusho 101
tantrums 48–49, 51–52
tardive dyskinesia 88–89
thalamus 42, 57–58, *63*
thinking, disorganized 22, 23
thyroid dysfunction 27
transsexualism 41
transvestites *41*
Treatment and Education of
   Autistic and related
   Communication-
   handicapped Children
   (TEACH) 53–54

U

unconditional positive regard 78

V

Valium 82

W

Wild Boy of Aveyron 50
withdrawal symptoms 37, 39,
   44–45

X

X chromosome 50